HUMAN SYSTEMS DYNAMICS INSTITUTE

Deep Learning Ecologies:
*An Invitation to
Complex Teaching and Learning*

by

Leslie Patterson
& Royce Holladay

*a guide for using
methods and models from
the field of human systems dynamics
to build learning ecologies for deep, systemic learning*

**An Invitation to
Complex Teaching and Learning**

© 2018 Human Systems Dynamics Institute. Use with permission.
Written by Leslie Patterson and Royce Holladay.
For permission, contact Royce Holladay at rholladay@hsdinstitute.org.

Printed in United States of America
ISBN-13: 978-0-9994202-0-1

Published by
Human Systems Dynamics Institute
50 East Golden Lake Road
Circle Pines, MN 55014
www.hsdinstitute.org
Phone: 866-HSD-INST

**An Invitation to
Complex Teaching and Learning**

Dear Reader,

We believe that learning, like growth in any living organism, emerges moment by moment, in sometimes surprising ways. Just as a healthy natural ecology supports growth of the organisms that live there, a healthy learning ecology supports individual and collective learning.

In these modules, and in the learning experiences they are designed to accompany, we explain how to set conditions for that kind of deep, organic learning and how to best sustain it over time. This approach to teaching and learning is grounded in human systems dynamics (HSD), a field of study that focuses on complex human systems.

Since 2000, when Glenda Eoyang began sharing her findings about how complex human systems work through the Human Systems Dynamics Institute, HSD has been used around the globe by practitioners in diverse fields such as medicine, social services, natural resource management, manufacturing, and education. HSD's compelling message is that human beings can deal with our most unpredictable and confounding challenges if we strive to see, understand, and influence the patterns emerging in our lives. We find this line of inquiry relevant to teaching and learning in K-12 schools because:

- ▶ HSD is action-oriented and inquiry-driven—integrating theory with practice to build adaptive capacity and to encourage patterns of resilience, courage, and joy.
- ▶ HSD concepts, methods, and models work for everyone in the system.
- ▶ HSD acknowledges difference as a potential source of energy in the system.
- ▶ HSD focuses on system assets, encouraging empathy and generative engagement across the whole.
- ▶ HSD views "learning" as "adaptation," which can ultimately lead individuals and systems to patterns of resilience and sustainability.

We thank Glenda Eoyang as the founder of the field of HSD and as our colleague and mentor in this work. All of the ideas in this book emerge from our applications of her work in teaching and learning. We also thank the colleagues who have stood beside us in this inquiry and whose stories bring the HSD ideas to life:

- ▶ Carol Wickstrom and other colleagues in the North Star of Texas Writing Project
- ▶ Wendy Gudalewicz and the administrators of the Cupertino Union School District
- ▶ Sabine Siekmann, Wendy Martelle, Joan Parker Webster, and the teachers in the Literacy for Emergent Bilinguals program at University of Alaska-Fairbanks.

We invite you into this network of teachers and learners, and we look forward to hearing how these ideas work in your school.

Leslie Patterson
(leslie.patterson@unt.edu)

Royce Holladay
(rholladay@hsdinstitute.org)

**An Invitation to
Complex Teaching and Learning**

Contents

Part 1: A Deep Dive into Deep Learning Ecologies i

Module 1 The Stance: Inquiry 1

    What challenges? 1

        Diversity 2

        Uncertainty 2

        Fragmentation 3

        Alienation, Disengagement, and Cynicism 3

    So what does HSD offer to address these challenges? 4

        Explanation Informs Action 4

        Two Competing Perspectives on Change 5

        Inquiry 8

    Now what will you do to frame your challenges? 9

Module 2 The Process: Adaptation 15

    What is a Complex Adaptive System? 15

        Complex Adaptive System: A Definition 16

        Complex Adaptive Systems: Coherence Across Scales 17

    What creates change in a Complex Adaptive System? 19

    So what does this mean in deep learning ecologies? 22

    Now what will emerge as you map your ecology? 22

Module 3 The System: Deep Learning Ecologies 25

    What is a deep learning ecology? 26

    What does an ecology require? 27

    So what makes these patterns emerge? 32

    Now what is your assessment of your own learning ecology? 35

Part 2: Applications: Models and Methods 41

Module 4 Your Action: See, Understand, and Influence 43

    What is Adaptive Action? 44

    What is Pattern Logic? 46

    What is the CDE Model? 48

    So what do we gain from CDE, PL, and AA together? 52

    So what do CDE, PL, and AA mean in schools? 53

    Now what? 54

Module 5 Praxis: Connect Theory and Practice 57

    What is praxis? 58

    So what integrates theory & practice in a deep learning ecology? 60

    Now what is your Praxis Triangle? 61

Module 6 Connect: Generative Engagements 65

    What are Generative Engagements? 65

    So what conditions shape Generative Engagements? 67

        Shared Identity 68

        Shared Power 70

        Shared Voice 71

        Non-generative Patterns of Engagement 72

        Generative Engagements for Adaptive Capacity 74

    Now what do you see in the Generative Engagements Model? 75

Module 7 Act: Set Conditions 77

    What conditions can we set? 77

    So what are the Four Big Questions for learning ecologies? 79

        Shared Identity 80

        Shared Learning Focus 82

        Differences that Matter 83

        Shared Practices 86

    Now what Four Big Questions inform your learning ecology? 88

Module 8 Act: Organize for Deep Learning 91

    What are deep learning cycles? 92

        What? *Explore* 93

        What? *Frame the Question or Challenge* 94

        What? *Gather Information* 95

        So What? *Search for Patterns* 96

        Now What? Design and Compose to Share the Learning 99

        Now What? Assess and Move On 100

    So what are deep learning cycles across the system? 101

    Now what shapes my deep learning cycle? 102

Module 9 Decision: When to Step in and When to Step Out 105

    What is just enough support for a learner? 105

    What is the Landscape Diagram? 107

    So what does this mean for a lead learner's decisions? 109

    Now what will the landscape be for your learning ecology? 114

Module 10 The Task: Build Coherence 115

    What are Simple Rules? 116

    So how do Simple Rules help build adaptive capacity for systemic change? ... 119

    Now how can you use Simple Rules to look back and move forward? 121

Appendix 125

References 127

    Books/Journals/Papers 127

    Websites 129

**An Invitation to
Complex Teaching and Learning**

Note:

We think that every individual in the system can and should teach and learn at various points in time. So, unless we are referring to a specific job in the system, we will use the "learner" and "lead learner" designations. As you read, you can think in terms of "students," "teachers," "administrators," or "stakeholders," depending on your context.

This book is written from the perspective of classroom teachers and school/district administrators. We believe the principles found here are transferable to any individual or group who wishes to set conditions for deep learning in any human system. If you work outside classrooms and want to set conditions for deep learning, consider the ways these principles, models, and methods support the work you do.

Part 1: A Deep Dive into Deep Learning Ecologies

Module 1
The Stance: Inquiry

Life is a process of working out what's not working for you and disentangling yourself from it and trying then not to walk into the same thing again. Watching your patterns and correcting them if you can.

Siobhan Fahey

School leaders—both teachers and administrators—are super heroes. They spend long hours with students. They help each one learn to read critically, to ask questions, to compose powerful messages, and to problem solve. They also help students build on the knowledge they bring from their homes and communities. They work to help students build identities, make sense of the world, set goals, and then take action toward those goals. Many of them are on call 24/7, answering e-mails, texts, and Tweets far beyond the end of the school day.

They do this work in a system that is constantly battered by multiple economic, social, and political forces. School leaders deal with increasing diversity—differences in race, gender, socio-economic status, culture, language, and family stability. They also have access to boundless information and misinformation that inform life in the 21st century.

That's not all. Teachers and school leaders also attend meetings, call parents, complete paperwork, align curriculum, review lesson plans, take graduate courses, attend community events, and reach out to policy makers. Then they go home to soccer games, family dinners, and laundry. When they are in the community, they are often seen—both formally and informally—as the "face of the school." So, what they say and do carries influence and responsibility.

What challenges?

Clearly, this chaotic work is fraught with challenges. After many years of teaching and leading at the campus and district levels, we know these challenges from the inside out. Here are a few of the most pressing challenges, with suggestions about how we can view each one in a more positive and generative way.

> **What challenges do you face as a lead learner in your school community?**

An Invitation to Complex Teaching and Learning

Diversity

Students need many kinds of support—physical, emotional, and academic. Each support is fine-tuned to meet an amazing range of diversities. These diversities pose significant challenges in large public schools. These schools are charged with meeting everyone's needs, and standardization promises both efficiency and effectiveness. Human systems dynamics (HSD), however, posits a positive approach to diversity. We join others who meet these diverse challenges with a sincere commitment to focus on strengths. We join those who help individual students mobilize their strengths to deal with risks facing their families and communities. We resist the widespread tendency of educators to frame diversity as a problem or deficit.

Dyson, an influential language and literacy researcher, points to the widespread persistence of deficit discourse as an "erasure of children's potential." She says that sociocultural approaches can "suggest that this erasure violates an old pedagogical truth. Teaching every child depends on knowledge of, respect for, and building on what that child knows and can do, to which I add, what that child, in the company of other children, feels, fears, and socially longs for (2015, p. 199)."

HSD practitioners treat diversity as a source of strength and a potential for change. We do not see it as an intractable problem to be solved.

Uncertainty

We believe that all our frenetic activity in schools is grounded in the best of intentions. It emerges in response to our fear of an uncertain future. Many families are in crisis. Resources are not equitable. Policies are always changing. The economy is unstable. Technology is shifting our cultural practices. Public institutions do not have the capacity to fulfill their promises. Struggles for power disrupt in violent acts, both unintended and intentional, both subtle and explicit. Each day brings new challenges as well as surprising twists on more familiar ones. Schools are uncertain places.

Typically, educators hope to manage and control their unpredictable environments. They don't know that uncertainty also holds the potential for change. In uncertainty, we find the space to ask questions, to make changes, and to consider options. Gilda Radner, a comedian who dealt with her share of uncertainties in life, said it this way:

> *I wanted a perfect ending. Now I've learned, the hard way, that some poems don't rhyme, and some stories don't have a clear beginning, middle, and end. Life is about not knowing, having to change, taking the moment and making the best of it, without knowing what's going to happen next.*
>
> *Delicious Ambiguity!*

HSD practitioners see uncertainty as "delicious ambiguity" where the patterns have not yet come clear. But in uncertainty, we can make the space to search for patterns, to make sense of our experiences, and to find options for action.

Fragmentation

In honest attempts to help students and teachers, educational policy makers have developed initiatives to target a range of issues. English learners, homeless students, learners with special needs, students whose families live in poverty have become the targets of dozens of separate initiatives. Administrators coordinate these programs, even as they manage facilities, food services, counseling, medical support, and community relations. Teachers' work is fragmented into 45-minute classes and six-week grading periods. It's punctuated by common assessments, pep rallies, and fundraisers. Teachers' professional learning opportunities are also fragmented. They attend workshops and institutes that focus on separate content areas and interventions.

Fullan claims that "coherence, then, is what is in the minds and actions of people individually and especially collectively" (Fullan, 2015) Life in schools does feel fragmented, but we can move toward coherence. That happens when we look for patterns across the fragments. This is especially true if we invite colleagues and students to identify patterns and use them as a basis for future action.

HSD practitioners take time to consider the array of what may, at first, seem to be disconnected initiatives or components in their systems. In those components, they search for the similarities—the underlying coherence across the fragmentation.

Alienation, Disengagement, and Cynicism

Each of these challenges—diversity, unpredictability, and fragmentation—separate teachers and administrators from one another. Educators are so busy they have little time for collaborative reflection and community building. Professional isolation can plant seeds of alienation that ultimately grow into disengagement. Weary teachers may greet each new initiative with guarded enthusiasm or with unabashed cynicism. Their experiences tell them the next superintendent will abandon this one and introduce yet another new and improved initiative. Over time, weary people withdraw. They move into a survival mode. When this happens in school, it is certainly not healthy for the children and young adults. Nor is it healthy for the organization, or for the educators themselves.

HSD practitioners work with others in the system to make sense of what is happening. They name what they see. Then they make decisions about what to do next. As we work to build coherence across programs and initiatives, we can also build relationships and a sense of belonging for adults and for students alike. That collaborative work and collective thinking can work against alienation and disengagement in schools today.

**An Invitation to
Complex Teaching and Learning**

So what does HSD offer to help us deal with these challenges?

So what does HSD offer to address these challenges?

Of course, heroic educators work to ensure that each student develops his or her unique potential. Hundreds of resources propose a multitude of solutions to address achievement gaps, lack of family involvement and community support, , limited resources, high stakes accountability schemes, and more.

So, what does human systems dynamics (HSD) add to this mix?

HSD offers methods and models, described in the modules below, that help educators think about the whole system at once. These methods and models help them take action to shift the larger system, no matter where they work in that system. HSD does not offer a range of isolated solutions to discrete problems. Instead, we offer a coherent vision of learning as adaptive and generative. We offer a vision that helps teachers and other schools leaders build a coherent, organic network of relationships among people, ideas, and artifacts. We offer an ecology nourished by the power of inquiry and adaptive learning. It's an ecology where effective programs and practices will grow and thrive in a coherent interdependence.

Explanation Informs Action

In the modules that follow, we offer a few flexible tools to help educators set conditions for a deep learning ecology. They help make the most of each teaching and learning moment, whether the learners are children, youth or adults. These methods and models can support concrete actions in specific situations. They work in service of adaptation and learning across the whole system. We call this whole-system learning "adaptive capacity," and we explain it more fully in Module 10.

These methods don't fragment educators' work across multiple initiatives. They help us focus on the patterns that hold these challenges together. They lead us to options for local action. At the same time, they also help educators stay mindful of the larger patterns emerging from the system. These larger patterns provide critical information, because they suggest how the underlying dynamics work. They also have the power to influence future actions, identities, and attitudes at the local level. In addition, those patterns suggest options for action with the potential to support learners across the system. Even small influences in these complex systems can influence larger trends and movements toward system-wide change (for good or for ill).

Often, school reformers cite systems approaches that merely base their claims on generalized descriptions of systems. For example, they point out that systems are in constant motion or that components are interdependent. From those descriptions, we can learn about systemic change and its attributes. We can learn what others have done in the face of similar challenges. Those descriptions, however, seldom include specific recommendations for how to identify and take action based on local conditions and needs.

HSD methods fill that gap by explaining the underlying systems dynamics and suggesting options for action for anyone in the system. More important, these methods are also models, in that they show how complex dynamics work. Each one contributes to a comprehensive theoretical framework, that can help users make responsive decisions in complex systems. This HSD perspective on theory and practice challenges the dominant perspective in schools today.

> **Descriptions:** Tell you what it looks like and/oe what it is doing
> **Explanations:** Tell you how it works!

Two Competing Perspectives on Change

A quick Internet search about K-12 education policy in the U.S. will generate a long list of articles that either praise or blame recent policy mandates. Many of these mandates attempt to improve student learning. They focus on accountability schemes, standardized testing, evidence-based practice, or performance-based teacher evaluation. All of those approaches are based on assumptions that learning is generally a linear process that can be reliably replicated across contexts. In other words, this is seen as a "common sense" approach (see Mayher, 1990). Here are some recommendations that may appear to be common sense, but which, we argue, do not support deep, organic learning:

- Find what is not working and fix it.
- Use high-stakes standardized testing to hold schools and educators accountable.
- Use measures of student learning to assess individual teacher performance.
- Identify "best practices" and replicate them in other contexts.
- Standardize curriculum and instruction to ensure rigor across the system.

These recommendations may make some sort of superficial sense, but they are based on a view of teaching and learning as a closed system. They consider teaching very much like a machine. It assumes that educators know precisely what content all children need to learn and how to make them learn it. It also assumes that learning proceeds uniformly, regardless of differences across contexts and between and among individual learners. This mechanistic perspective assumes teachers and administrators should build structures and implement methods to help students reach pre-determined objectives. That approach also leads the entire education system to depend on standardized tests and "teacher-proof" instructional programs to guide teaching and learning.

Educators have long critiqued this mechanistic perspective (for example, Higgins, 2014; Renzuli, 2012). Many have argued that human learning does not work like a machine or a factory. They describe it more like an organism or an ecosystem. In fact, in HSD we join others around the world who have rejected mechanistic assumptions for more open-ended approaches to teaching and learning. These include early childhood educators, like those who ascribe to student-centered,

An Invitation to Complex Teaching and Learning

problem-solving Montessori and the Reggio Emelia approaches. They also include educators advocating an emphasis on STEM as a "way to understand and explore and engage with the world, and then have the capacity to change that world. . ." (Obama, 2015). Additionally, literacy educators argue that literacy is a disciplinary practice through which students can influence their worlds. Sugata Mitra and his colleagues use SOLE (self-organizing learning environments) as a dramatic example of this general movement away from a mechanistic perspective toward a nonlinear approach to teaching and learning (2013).

Although these educators and researchers may use different language from HSD, our perspective is similar. We view human systems as open, diverse, and nonlinear. We describe the work of systems as building resilience by being sensitive to internal and external conditions and responding to those conditions to find greatest coherence and fit. This is how we believe our educational institutions should function to support learners. They should help build skills to function in their own families and communities as they grow.

We do not suggest that mechanistic approaches are absolutely wrong, or that organic approaches are always appropriate. Educators know that, in the daily reality of schools, absolutes don't serve well. It works better to think in terms of "interdependent pairs"—where two extremes are in a constant, dynamic tension with one another.

Table 1.1 represents the interdependent pairs that emerge in the contrasting educational perspectives. It also includes some implications for issues related to teaching and learning. In an ideal world, we might wish for a completely organic perspective toward all challenges in schools. Given the challenges currently facing school leaders, some decisions (safety, payroll, memorization, etc.) require a more efficient use of time and resources. Those functions can use a more mechanistic perspective, with few degrees of freedom. On the other hand, some decisions should be more open-ended.

These interdependent pairs do not offer an "either-or" choice between mutually exclusive perspectives. For us, it poses a question of whether the decision fits the situation. We encourage school leaders to adjust their approaches to fit the system's immediate function, in the context of long-range goals. Additionally, we encourage policy makers and the larger community to understand that educators can have the information, skill, and professionalism to make those choices in their day-to-day decision making. This chart is meant as a thinking tool to help us imagine practical implications of each of these perspectives.

Clearly, this approach moves us beyond either-or thinking to consider the context and purpose of specific tasks. We argue that most decisions directly related to teaching and learning will move toward the organic end of the continuum.

Table 1.1. Two opposing views of change in schools.

Implications for ...	Mechanistic View *(complicated)*		Organic View *(complex)*
Purpose of Instruction	reinforce & replicate familiar patterns	↕	invite exploration, noticing, & naming patterns
Teaching Practices	control learning by target tasks/content; provide info & models; guide learners	↕	support/mediate learning by noticing, interpreting, & influencing patterns
Teacher's Role	control learning as expert & "reinforcer"	↕	provide support that fits learner; as resource & co-learner
Learners' Role	replicate models; find correct answers	↕	generate possible answers & new questions
Policy Making	standardize teaching & assessment	↕	build coherence; ensure flexibility in response to local needs
Nature of Change	trust linear cause-effect relationships	↕	expect unpredictable & emergent processes
Motivation	use external rewards & incentives reinforce desired behaviors	↕	leverage self-organizing dynamics within individuals & groups to influence transformation
Metaphor for Learning Environment	rely on assembly line	↕	set conditions for an ecology of deep learning

An Invitation to Complex Teaching and Learning

Human systems dynamics suggests that informed and thoughtful educators can take appropriate action. The methods and models presented in the following modules will help school leaders do just that. In general, the more specific advice in the modules can be boiled down to these three steps:

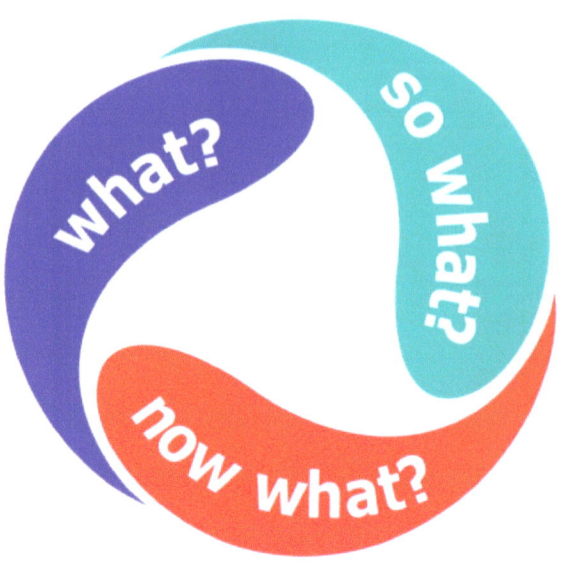

- Ask: **What?**
    - Take an inquiry stance.
    - Search for patterns in your systems.
- Ask: **So What?**
    - Make sense of the patterns.
    - Look for new options for action.
- Ask: **Now What?**
    - Take action most likely to influence those patterns.
    - Generate new questions.

Figure 1.1. Adaptive Action

HSD calls this process **Adaptive Action**.

Inquiry

Teachers and other school leaders who take a complex perspective invite colleagues and students to find creative ways to deal with challenges. Together they use inquiry and Adaptive Action to transform themselves, their communities, and the world.

Inquiry is the heart of deep learning and the promise of transformation. What do we mean by inquiry? Of course, it's about asking questions and looking for answers. We have found a more concrete definition of inquiry that names four stances we can take.

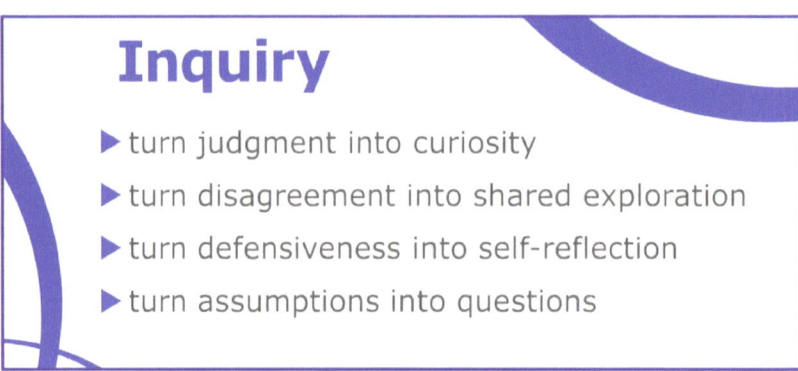

Figure 1.2. HSD Definition of Inquiry

These four guidelines make "inquiry" more concrete and bring inquiry to life. They can provide useful reminders in all areas of our lives. In classrooms and schools, these guidelines can help us stand in inquiry as we try to work. In other words, inquiry is a hallmark of deep learning that can become a way of life.

Inquiry and deep learning become both the product and the process. They are the destination and the path. Educators can use inquiry and deep learning in a number of ways:

- Help identify personal and professional goals
- Set priorities
- Make instructional decisions
- Build relationships with students
- Collaborate with colleagues and community members
- Develop curriculum
- Advocate for our students.

Inquiry and deep learning throughout system will help us all feel more confident and hopeful as we face each surprising day in schools.

We also need to remember that humility is important for those of us who want to see, understand, and influence patterns in schools. We try to remember that ours is just one of many possible perspectives. We are open to a range of alternatives that prove both true and useful in complex learning environments. Humility means that we always work in inquiry. We listen to multiple perspectives. We take action. We watch closely to see the influence of our actions.

Now what will you do to frame your challenges?

So what about those challenges we described at the beginning of this module—diversity, uncertainty, fragmentation, and alienation? Together and individually, we can study the concrete details of our challenges and frame our questions for inquiry. Consider how each of the following challenges can be framed as a "how" or "why" question.

> **Now what can you see in your challenges?**

An Invitation to Complex Teaching and Learning

Challenge

Elementary Teacher: "This year, in my third-grade class of 26 students, two families are going through divorces, one child's mother just finished breast cancer treatment, three children have parents who are job hunting, and two families have moved to this country within the last couple years. Many of my children's families are in transition, and mostly for unhappy reasons. There is no way I can meet all their needs!"

Questions for Inquiry

- How can I build strong and trusting relationships with these children and their families?
- How can I provide a safe place for these children whose lives outside of school are unpredictable and, in some cases, dangerous?
- How do I balance my attention to their emotional needs with my attention to their academic progress?
- **What else?**

Challenge

Middle School Teacher: "I'm ready to give up. I have tried every thing I know to motivate some of my students, and they simply do not want to read or write. Maybe they think they can't. Maybe they are embarrassed to show any enthusiasm in front of their friends. How can they improve if they don't even try? I don't know what to do."

Questions for Inquiry

- What are they thinking? How to get them to express feelings about this? What is their basis of resistance?
- How do people use reading and writing in community? What real purposes inform classroom literacy work?
- How can I extend, enrich my literacy experiences so I can talk to students about my joys and challenges as a reader and as an author?
- **What else?**

Challenge

Superintendent: "My school is in a village on the Yukon River, and the people in the community want to preserve and revitalize their language, but they also know that, for their children, English is the language of success and power outside the village. I feel frustrated about these opposing goals and am at a loss about what I can do—especially with the need to raise test scores on the English-only test."

Questions for Inquiry

- How do people learn languages? Is it different for native languages & for additional language people might learn?
- How can I best honor and support village culture and language while I also help students learn to use English for academic and career purposes?
- How can I invite students to become "language detectives" to notice and investigate similarities and differences across languages?
- **What else?**

Challenge

Elementary School Principal: "Half of my faculty are early career teachers. They are concerned and committed, but inexperienced. Each year, it seems that we have new initiatives—for math or reading or talented/gifted or English learners. They need intensive support for these new initiatives, but also for basic issues like behavior management and differentiation. Our resources for professional learning are stretched to the breaking point, and it's still not enough."

Questions for Inquiry

- How can I invite and encourage our experienced faculty members to share their expertise in a systematic way?
- How can I make time to get into classrooms to offer my encouragement and support?
- How can we identify and highlight faculty strengths and successes?
- What do faculty members see as the most challenging barriers to strong instruction?
- **What else?**

An Invitation to Complex Teaching and Learning

Challenge

High School Teacher: "Every year I have more students who have just moved to this country and have to take the state tests in English within a year. They are working hard, and their English is improving quickly, but the test is looming! Research says people take five to seven years to learn a language well enough to pass a test like this, and these students have less than a year to prepare! It's not fair to them—or to me."

Questions for Inquiry

- How can I best support these students and accelerate their language learning?
- How can I balance the need to emphasize test preparation with other critical learning goals for these students?
- Why do policy makers think that these students need to face this challenge? How can I convince them that newly arrived students should not be expected to pass a high-stakes test so soon?
- **What else?**

Frame your challenges as questions.

Try one here:

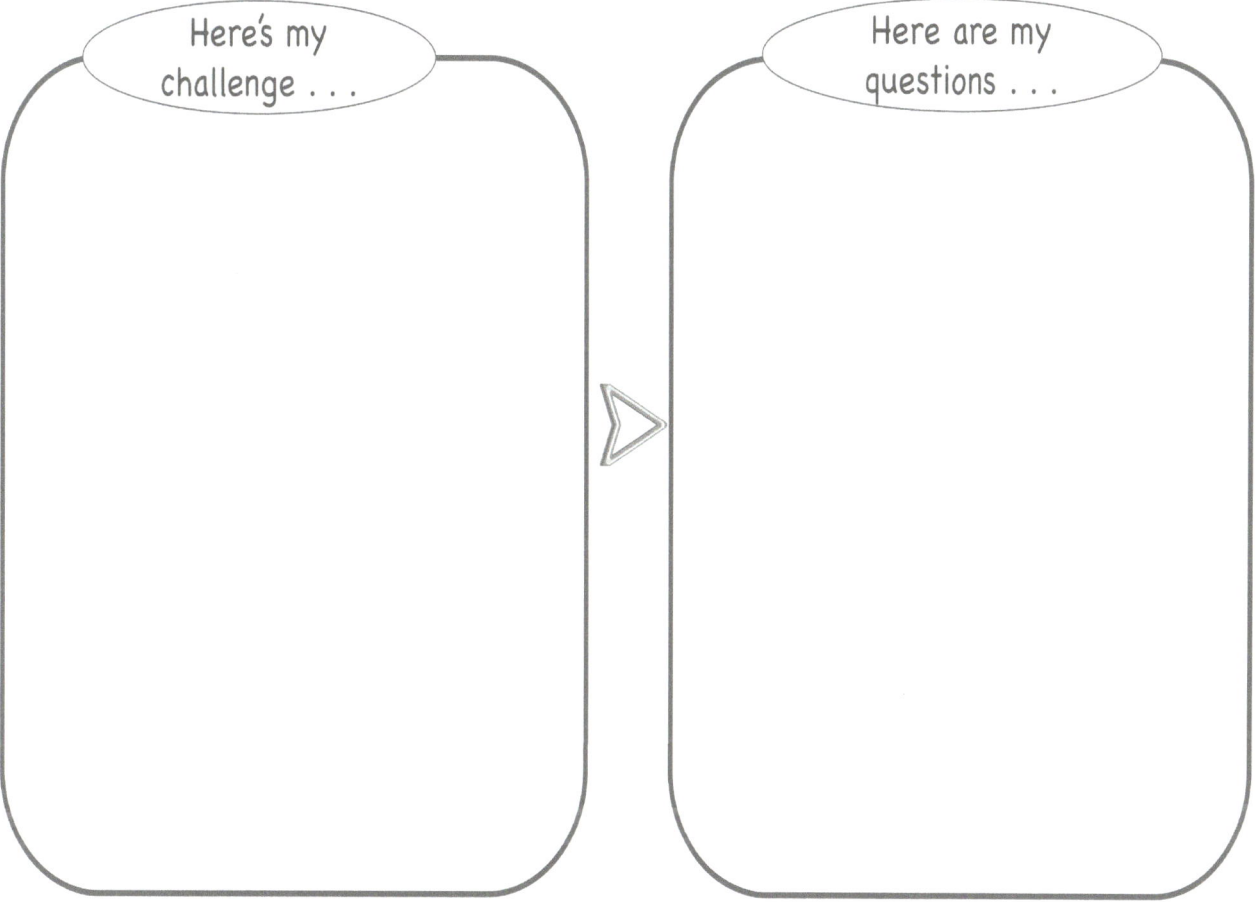

**An Invitation to
Complex Teaching and Learning**

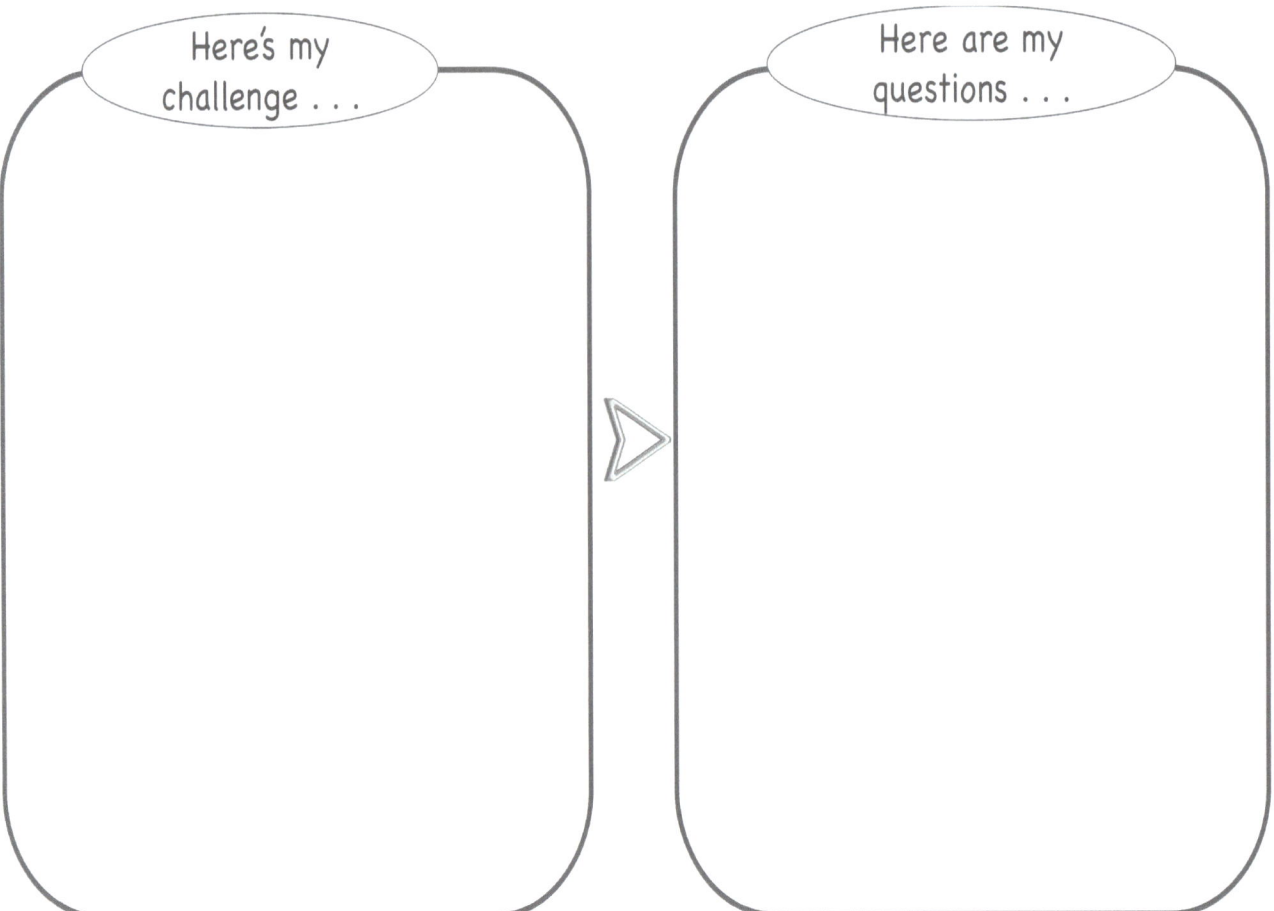

Module 2
The Process: Adaptation

We who engage in nonviolent direct action are not the creators of tension. We merely bring to the surface the hidden tension that is already alive.

Martin Luther King, Jr.

Human systems are full of surprises, puzzles, conflicts, and challenges. There are too many interdependent parts that simply will not stand still long enough for anyone to understand all that might be happening. Schools are particularly complex because:

- ▶ Multiple forces shape the reality in public education
- ▶ Diversities such as age, interests, languages, socio-economic status, culture, gender
- ▶ Traditions and expectations dictate how schools should function.

What makes human systems so complex?

No matter how much you plan or rehearse, you can neither predict nor control these systems or the human beings within them.

What is a Complex Adaptive System?

Scientists from many different fields have studied complex systems—the weather, wave action, the human body, to name a few. Across these diverse phenomena, scientists point to a number of common characteristics (for example, Cilliers, 1998). In our work, we found three characteristics of complex systems to be particularly useful in explaining why human systems are so challenging. These systems have:

- ▶ Open boundaries
- ▶ Diverse components or participants
- ▶ Non-linear connections or relationships

What creates complexity in a system?
- ▶ Open boundaries
- ▶ High diversity
- ▶ Nonlinear relationships

Taken together, these characteristics mean that interactions among individuals on the campus are connected and interdependent. They also can grow more

An Invitation to Complex Teaching and Learning

interconnected over time. Each individual is unique. Particular relationships are unique. The connections that exist mean that the whole system takes on a life of its own. They "self-organize" to form a whole that emerges from all the interdependent parts. As a whole, the classroom community is different from the combination of its parts. Systems scientists call this "emergence". They see new, more complex patterns of behavior emerge from interactions among the various agents of the system. That's the source of surprises, puzzles, conflicts, and challenges in human systems. Surprising patterns of behavior emerge from these complex interactions among people, ideas, materials, and tools.

Complex Adaptive System: A Definition

Dooley (1996), who has studied complex systems primarily in business organizations, uses three interdependent features to define a CAS (Figure 3.1):

▶ A set of agents (people, groups, ideas) that interact

▶ System-wide patterns emerge from those interactions

▶ The strongest patterns influence subsequent interactions among the agents

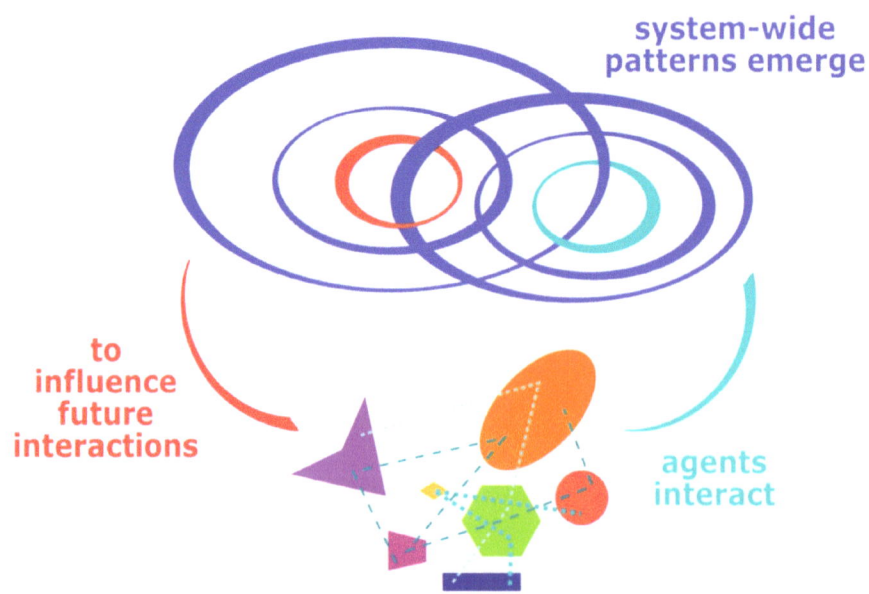

Figure 2.1. Emergent patterns in a complex adaptive system (CAS)

As you can see in Figure 2.1, the individual actors (students, and the adults around them) are represented by the small ovals and circles at the bottom. They interact with each other. These "actors" may also be inanimate objects or abstractions—like curricular mandates, texts, and resources. As they interact, system-wide patterns emerge (represented by the ovals at the top of Figure 2.1). These patterns are sometimes welcome, but not always. These emergent patterns—like trust, inquiry, or compliance—may be judged as either positive or negative, depending on whether they fit the system's function. They are judged by the degree to which they help the system adapt to various forces.

It is important to notice the patterns you see in learning ecologies. You also need to think about whether those patterns fit the system's function. Think, for example, about a pattern of compliance. In a fire drill, you want compliance. In a creative writing class, you don't. The patterns that become dominant over time constrain the system in particular ways. For better or worse, they set up expectations or parameters for future interactions of the participants.

For instance, if compliance during fire drill procedures is not emphasized and enforced, you see chaotic and less predictable behaviors. If you don't take action to reinforce compliance, students begin to act as though individual action is acceptable when the fire alarm goes off. Clearly, that pattern would not fit the function of a fire drill.

We have focused in this module on a learning ecology as a single complex adaptive system. It is clear that, within a school, there are many nested and overlapping complex adaptive systems at work. Consider individual learners, grade-level teams, families, content-area teams, and on and on. These systems and subsystems are linked and interdependent. Here are three examples:

- Physiological and neurological systems within each human act together. They digest food, fight infection, and process information. They control our body functions, depending on the conditions that exist in their bodies at any given time.

- Social systems like friendship groups, families, and neighborhoods, emerge from the interactions between and among the individuals and groups who are connected. The dominant patterns of interdependence become the cultural patterns that characterize those individual systems or groups.

- Political and economic systems like social classes and political parties are formed through the shared activities of people who share ideological perspectives.

Complex Adaptive Systems: Coherence Across Scales

Murray Gell-Mann, a Noble Laureate in physics, has said that everything—even the universe itself—is a complex adaptive system:

> *Whether putting together a business plan for a new venture, adapting a recipe, or learning a language, you are behaving as a complex adaptive system. If you are training a dog, you are watching a complex adaptive system in operation, and you are functioning as one as well (if it is mainly the latter that is happening, then the dog may be training you, as is often the case.).*
>
> *(1994, p.19)*

To do their jobs, educators need to focus on various scales. For example, even a single classroom holds complex adaptive processes at several scales:

- Each individual learner has ideas, concepts, and understandings that form patterns of learning. Those patterns hold the potential for shaping new knowledge and insights.

An Invitation to Complex Teaching and Learning

- ▶ Groups of students interact with each other to form patterns that shape the class climate and culture.

- ▶ The students and teacher interaction create patterns of learning and interaction that shape and inform future actions.

- ▶ Administrators and the staff in a building work together to shape the campus culture over time.

The fact that these multiple scales are interdependent and linked in nonlinear relationships helps explain how systems change. Tension builds in one system as differences "bump" against each other. The system shifts to relieve the increasing tension and triggers movement or self-organization. It shifts the balance of tension in other nearby, interdependent and similarly nested systems. Those nearby systems shift to relieve that tension.

Figure 2.2. In schools, multiple complex adaptive systems continually work with and on each other.

When school and school district leaders understand that learning systems are complex in this way, they know that nothing is certain. They can neither predict nor control the emergent patterns they experience. But they can do something. They can watch for patterns. They strive to understand those patterns. Then they take action to influence those patterns to support learners at all scales of their systems. This is the process HSD calls Adaptive Action. It is the iterative inquiry cycle introduced in Module 1 that poses three basic questions:

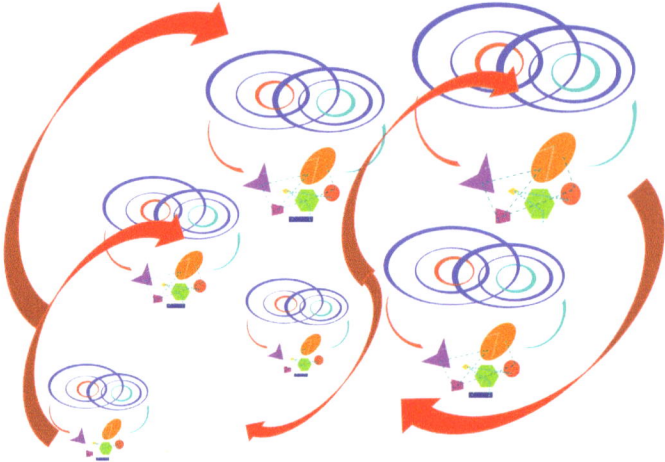

- ▶ **What** patterns do we see?

- ▶ **So what** do those patterns mean?

- ▶ **Now what** shall we do to create the patterns we want to see?

In a complex adaptive system, these emergent patterns are happening all around, whether you pay attention or not. A young boy's school pictures from one year to the next represent, in a series of snapshots, his physical changes across time. If you follow that student around for a year, you can capture those changes in a video. You would understand much more about subtle day-to-day changes that contribute to the growth over the year.

When you look at learners and schools as complex adaptive systems, think of what it means to watch a video instead of looking at a stack of snapshots. Notice the shifting patterns over time and how those changes happen. You may ask about how change happens in a complex adaptive system.

What creates change in a Complex Adaptive System?

What gives a complex adaptive system the energy to drive these changing patterns? To answer this question, scientists point to the tension that builds in the system when the parts do not fit together smoothly. When there is a lack of fitness or coherence, either between elements of the system, tension builds. It increases the chance the system will somehow shift to reduce the tension. Think, for example, of friction in a fan that needs to be lubricated. Tension builds between the parts of the machine. You hear it creak. You see it vibrate. In time, you see it stop running.

> **What triggers change in a complex human system?**

The word *tension*, in lay terms, is connected with negative emotions. In HSD, we use it more neutrally. For example, tension in a taut bungee cord holds a load of firewood in place. This kind of tension can be thought of as contained or controlled energy. In human systems, tension sometimes surfaces as curiosity or surprise, and sometimes as worry or anger. Here are examples of tension in learning ecologies:

- ▶ Teachers and students may feel tension when their performance doesn't match expectations. This is experienced either as disappointment or as determination to accomplish more next time.

- ▶ Children feel tension when they feel different from their peers. They experience either embarrassment about or pride in their unique qualities.

- ▶ Teachers and students feel tension in the difference between what they currently know and what they need or want to learn. This manifests as frustration or as curiosity.

- ▶ Administrators feel the tension between budget requests and the district's financial resources. They see this either as an overwhelming challenge or as an opportunity to seek new resources.

- ▶ You may feel the tension between what you expect and what you actually perceive. You feel this either as shock and surprise or as a reason to laugh out loud. The phrase "comic relief" is about the laughter that comes when tension builds to the point of release.

Tension also may build in the differences between those who have power and those who don't. It builds in the differences between assumptions or expectations related to race, gender, sexual preference, or class. In human systems, tension is always present. It is always central to our work and play. Tension is the first step toward transformation.

An Invitation to Complex Teaching and Learning

The important point for our work in learning ecologies is that systems respond to tension by self-organizing—by shifting in unpredictable ways to relieve the tension. In human systems, for example, curiosity can build to the point that you decide to look for an answer to your questions. Or frustration builds until you explode in anger. Some level of tension is essential to functioning systems because it concentrates energy. That energy that holds the potential to fuel systemic change.

Tension! Internal energy that results from a lack of system coherence and drives change in a complex adaptive system

A system without tension is stagnant, even to the point of death. Tension triggers the system's underlying dynamic. Tension can drive adaptation. In a school, you can think of that adaptation as learning. As a participants within the system, you cannot predict how your system will change in response to this growing tension. Neither can you predict whether you will experience the changes as positive or negative. The best you can do is to be aware of the tensions triggered by differences among our past, current, and hoped-for realities. As you take note of those tensions and surrounding patterns, you can make sense of what is happening. Then you can take action that is most likely to release tension and trigger movement toward your goals.

HSD practitioners try to avoid labeling a particular decision or action as absolutely "good" or "bad." Instead, we focus on a particular action and then zoom out to the whole system. From that vantage, we can discern how well the action "fits." In other words, we look to see whether that action is likely to increase coherence or alignment in the larger system. On the other hand, we look at the degree and direction it might shift tension.

Many challenges educators face happen because tensions at one scale are building and being released differently across parts of the system. An individual third grader, may reduce tension within his personal system by slamming his book down on the table. This can cause unwanted tension among his classmates, who are all reading quietly. The change that fit one part of system caused tension in closely related parts. That change, in turn, builds tension elsewhere.

One characteristic of complex systems is that tensions shift at multiple scales in response to tensions between and among the parts of the larger system. These nonlinear dynamics between, among, and within the diverse parts in a system are particularly challenging in human systems like schools. They also make life in schools intriguing and, sometimes, entertaining!

In Table 2.1, we imagine some examples of tensions that can build within schools.

Table 2.1 Tensions that build in schools

Ask . . .	Explore possible answers . . .	Identify tensions . . .
Who or what interacts over time?	▶ Students? ▶ Teachers? ▶ Administrators? ▶ Families? ▶ Curricular mandates? ▶ Programs? ▶ Tests? ▶ Community resources? . . . What else?	▶ Between students' current achievement and what is expected on state tests? ▶ Among individuals' various cultural knowledge and expectations?
What patterns have you noticed?	▶ Trust? ▶ Competition? ▶ Curiosity? ▶ Innovation? ▶ Compliance? ▶ Fear . . . What else?	▶ Between and among students' various identities or stances? ▶ Among the ends and means of particular instructional programs?
How have those patterns worked to influence or constrain subsequent interactions?	▶ Support or subvert shared goals? ▶ Encourage or diminish curiosity? ▶ Invite or discourage diverse voices? . . . What else?	▶ Between the time students need and the time available for instruction? . . .What else?

An Invitation to Complex Teaching and Learning

So what does this mean in deep learning ecologies?

So what about tension in a deep learning ecology?

Think, for a minute, about how this explanation of tensions within a complex adaptive system might fit your classroom or your team of colleagues. Actors in a classroom interact to generate tensions that shape combinations of system-wide patterns. The classroom culture develops. Over time, the norms and expectations of that culture begin to influence the behaviors of others by reinforcing behaviors that match the culture or by punishing or ignoring behaviors that don't fit.

Particular behaviors and attitudes are established as the "norm," are repeated and strengthened over time. Educators, wherever they work in the school system, can pay attention to these interactions, as well as the patterns that emerge. Through their messages and their actions, they can shape the emerging patterns. Figure 2.3 poses questions that can help you analyze your system and make conscious decisions about how to influence the speed, direction, and nature of system change.

These questions are useful for everyone in the system. Think of how these questions might work for a teacher working with an unruly group of third graders or for a superintendent planning for a potentially confrontational meeting with union representatives.

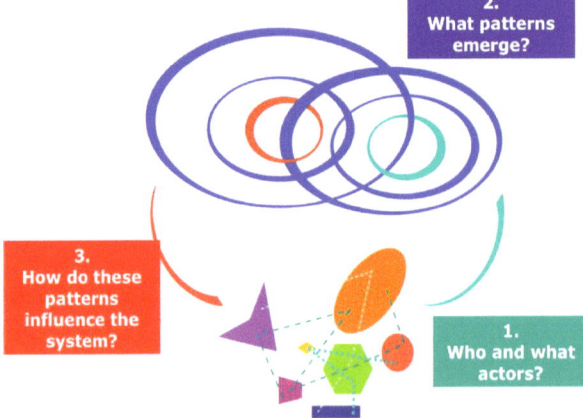

Figure 2.3. Questions for reflection about your deep learning ecology.

Now what will emerge as you map your ecology?

Map Your Classroom Ecology

As you explore the complex system where you work, use these questions to analyze:

Now what will your current map look like?

- ▶ Critical components or actors
- ▶ The dominant patterns
- ▶ Potential influence these patterns may have on system change.

Who are the actors in your ecology?

What are the critical documents, texts, or ideas?

How do these actors interact?

What are the differences that generate tension—either good or bad?

What patterns do you see emerging from these interactions and tensions?

Which patterns contribute to the learning? Which patterns disrupt the learning?

How do these patterns influence subsequent interactions and tensions in the system?

Module 3
The System:
Deep Learning Ecologies

I am lucky to work in a space where I glance up from my computer and look out at a lakeside ecology populated with trees, grasses, reeds, and flowering plants. My little slice of the world also teams with wild life. The birds are diverse—ducks, geese, herons, eagles, crows, hawks, owls, jays, and song birds fill the air. Mammals—squirrels, cats and dogs, and the occasional raccoon—seem to engage in endless games of chase and hide-and-go-seek. The mandatory collection of frogs, toads, turtles, and other amphibians and reptiles plays along the shore. In the spring and fall, we even get a few deer and foxes wandering through. At this time of year, the scene transitions from a lush, busy summer toward the quieter ecology of a frozen lake in the Minnesota winter. I marvel at the patterns of life that play themselves out in our backyard to create a generative, thriving ecology.

R. Holladay

The concept of ecological complexity stresses the richness of ecological systems and their capacity for adaptation and self-organization.

Li

Ecologies in the natural world, like rain forests, prairies, and wetlands, are alive and complex. They are made up of diverse, yet interdependent, elements. They are always changing. They continually evolve, as they adapt to shifting conditions. Sometimes they evolve in surprising ways. System-wide patterns emerge from the interactions of individual plants and animals in each particular environment. This means that no two ecologies are alike. Across categories of ecologies, we can see important similarities in how they function. Each rain forest is unique. At the same time, it is similar to other rain forests in significant ways.

Does that description sound something like a kindergarten classroom?

- ▶ Diverse group of children
- ▶ In relationship with one another and their teacher
- ▶ Always changing in response to shifting conditions in physical well-being, home lives, and the school context
- ▶ Changes are unpredictable and surprising
- ▶ Each classroom is unique, but similar in significant developmental patterns

An Invitation to Complex Teaching and Learning

HSD practitioners view all human systems as complex adaptive systems. By definition, this means they are ecologies. We established that classrooms are complex adaptive systems. So, when we focus on teaching and learning, HSD practitioners strive to set conditions for "deep learning ecologies."

What is a deep learning ecology?

> **What shapes a deep learning ecology?**

By "deep learning," we mean *"generative, adaptive, and creative learning grounded in both individual and collaborative inquiry."*

When educators are learners, they can deal with uncertainty. They ask insightful questions. They problem-solve. They know their disciplines and research traditions. They pay attention to their feelings, their insights, and their strategies. They know, maybe implicitly, that human systems are open, diverse, and unpredictable. They observe how complex systems work. They know that learning is a spiraling process of inquiry, reflection, and action. They also recognize benefits of collaborative inquiry inside a community. They use curricular standards in their planning. At the same time, they aren't driven by those standards or by high-stakes tests. They know each insight is not likely to lead not to an absolute answer. Rather it is likely to lead to an array of more interesting questions.

Clearly, a healthy and self-sustaining "ecology" can serve as an evocative metaphor. In a powerful teaching and learning system students, teachers, books, technology, and materials interact, and learning emerges in surprising ways!

We look to ecologists for more detail about these complex systems:

> *Ecological complexity refers to the complex interplay between all living systems and their environment, and emergent properties from such an intricate interplay. The concept of ecological complexity stresses the richness of ecological systems and their capacity for adaptation and self-organization. The complex, nonlinear interactions (behavioral, biological, chemical, ecological, environmental, physical, social, cultural) that affect, sustain, or are influenced by all living systems, including humans.*
>
> *Li*

As we see it, this description of ecological complexity in nature also captures the complexity of a supportive and generative learning system. Natural ecologies and deep learning ecologies are shaped by specific conditions. They are:

- ▶ **Open** – Complex systems have permeable boundaries and are open to multiple forces that act from inside the system and external to the system.

- ▶ **Diverse** – Differences among elements in a system hold tension. That tension generates energy to change the system.

- ▶ **Nonlinear** – Diverse elements (people, texts, and/or ideas) interact. Output from one set of interactions becomes feedback/input for a next interaction. This influences continuously transformation in future iterations.

These conditions shape the complexity of a system. They contribute to both the dynamism and ongoing transformation of the system. Sometimes the change is gradual and slow. Sometimes it is abrupt and surprising. In an ecology, no two days, no two moments, are the same. As a result, the current moment is all that's available for action. You cannot change the past. Nor can you predict or control the future. All you can do is

- Learn from your experiences.
- Imagine a more resilient and sustainable future.
- Choose action in the moment to move toward that future. (Eoyang and Holladay, 2014)

What does an ecology require?

Another way to think about the complex and emergent nature of a deep learning ecology is to look at the requirements for the growth of an ecosystem. What does it take for an ecosystem to function and to grow? What patterns might you see in a healthy learning ecology?

> **What patterns define a learning ecology?**

Ecologies in the natural world self-organize to sustain themselves as long as they can respond to existing conditions. Each ecology exists in this moment, as a product of the past. It adapts as the environment changes. Ecologists talk about four requisites for healthy and self-sustaining ecosystems. Consider these four requisites in the culture of the system where you live, work, or play. As you read about the four requisites, consider how they shape the world around you.

Diversity: Complex systems are made up of differing patterns of life and activity. Examples include: 1) water, air, and land; 2) rain, sun, light, and dark; 3) high activity and times of rest; 4) mammals, birds, amphibians, reptiles, insects; and 5) grasses, reeds, shrubs, flowers, and trees. As you build deep learning ecologies, you nurture diversity in multiple ways. Children bring differences of thought, learning needs, and experiences. Your instruction uses diverse materials, ideas, and stories to address those differences. Whether you are face-to-face or in virtual space, you bring as much diversity as possible to enhance learning experiences. In learning ecologies, you might:

- Ask questions
- Offer a wide variety of readings of multiple genre, modes, and perspectives
- Invite individual, personal responses, each of which would be unique
- Invite new people into the conversation
- Invite learners to respond to open-ended questions in multiple modes

An Invitation to Complex Teaching and Learning

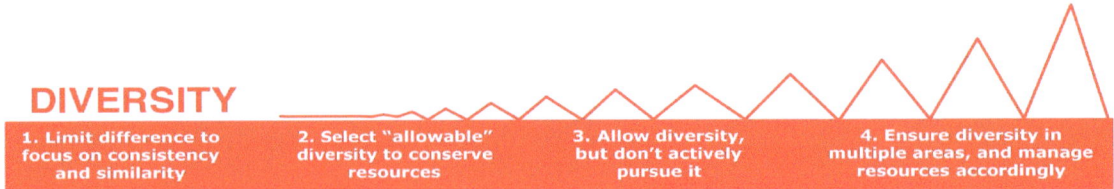

DIVERSITY

| 1. Limit difference to focus on consistency and similarity | 2. Select "allowable" diversity to conserve resources | 3. Allow diversity, but don't actively pursue it | 4. Ensure diversity in multiple areas, and manage resources accordingly |

Briefly, how would you characterize diversity—of all kinds—in your classroom? On your campus? Across your district? Within your learning team?

Take a few minutes to jot down your thoughts about the **diversity** in the system you want to explore.

Coherence: In deep learning ecologies, diverse learners come together, across a variety of shared spaces, topics, and applications. Deep learning emerges in your classrooms when the learners bring those diverse backgrounds together to coordinate and learn from each other. They innovate in the moment and learning from shared experiences. Deep learning emerges when you focus on those forces you can influence and build coherence to stand against those you cannot influence. Your learning ecologies set conditions that build coherence across the whole setting. They engage learners in high quality, action-oriented experiences. In learning ecologies, you might:

▶ Focus on similarities among learners by emphasizing shared identities, goals, and knowledge

▶ Focus on collaborative tasks

▶ Make collective learning goals and assumptions explicit

▶ Revisit your decisions occasionally to adjust or revise

▶ Build consensus about a set of simple rules to frame how the group members agree to work together

COHERENCE

| 1. Encourage individuality and self-expression without constraints of shared vision | 2. Encourage separate identities, within named boundaries | 3. Encourage similar identities without shaping specific decisions | 4. Share vision and Simple Rules to inform decisions within a coherent whole |

Briefly, how would you characterize coherence—in your classroom? On your campus? Across your district? Within your learning team?

Do you notice shared identities? Common beliefs and values? Shared focus or goals?

Take a few minutes to jot down your thoughts about the **coherence** in the system you want to explore.

Adaptive Capacity: In the northern hemisphere, winter approaches, and the days get shorter. The average daily temperature falls, and the ecology adapts. Squirrels stock their stores and put on their winter coats. Last year's fawns have grown stronger, ready for difficulties of a long winter. Trees shed leaves, and reeds at the edge of the lake die away.

In the same way, you support learners as they adapt to new ideas and build skills. You build adaptive capacity by helping everyone in the system to notice, name, interpret, and influence patterns that emerge in their systems. You adapt your support and conversation, depending on the type of course, the quality of the environment, and learners' interests and needs. You teach and learn, building capacity across the system. In learning ecologies, you might:

- Use a multiple data sources to make sense of what happens for individual learners and throughout the system
- Search for persistent patterns in the data
- Reflect on whether and why those patterns show progress or growth
- Consider actions that are most likely to shape those patterns in healthy and productive ways
- Encourage and support these inquiry, reflection, and decision-making processes for everyone in the system—for moment-by-moment decisions and for longer term planning

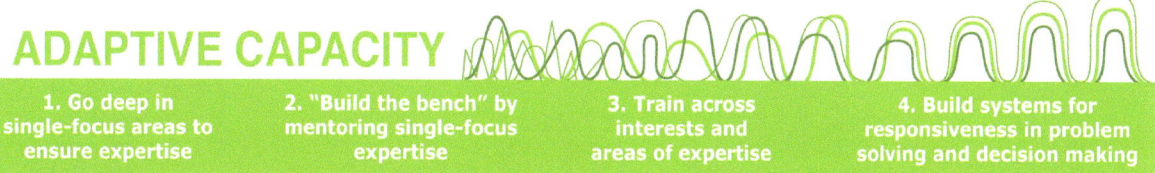

| 1. Go deep in single-focus areas to ensure expertise | 2. "Build the bench" by mentoring single-focus expertise | 3. Train across interests and areas of expertise | 4. Build systems for responsiveness in problem solving and decision making |

Briefly, how would you characterize Adaptive Capacity (seeing, understanding and influencing patterns)—in your classroom? On your campus? Across your district? Within your learning team?

To what extent do people document and analyze their experiences, as in the use of formative and summative student assessments? To what extent do they interpret what what information might mean to their practice? To what extent do they use their insights to inform their work?

An Invitation to Complex Teaching and Learning

Take a few minutes to jot down your thoughts about the **adaptive capacity** in the system you want to explore.

Interdependence: In an ecology, each part relies on other parts. These systems are open to multiple forces that

- ▶ Keep the water clean—or not
- ▶ Bring the rain—or not
- ▶ Nurture green spaces in the face of growing urban sprawl—or not
- ▶ Bring disease—or not

The ecology's character is influenced by choices and decisions of humans who also inhabit the ecology.

In deep learning ecologies, we bring diverse learners, ideas, and learning experiences together. The purpose is to support a resilient and interdependent community. In that community, individuals, and groups use what they learn to accomplish shared goals. In learning ecologies, we might:

- ▶ Encourage empathy
- ▶ Invite multiple perspectives on controversial issues
- ▶ Look for connections
- ▶ Support respectful conversations about significant issues
- ▶ Make similarities and connections explicit when possible
- ▶ Encourage everyone to consider the parts and the whole, and how each part influences and is influenced by the rest of the system

   **INTERDEPENDENCE**

| 1. Ensure efficiency by having people focus on their own work | 2. Connect people between parts of the system that work together | 3. Ensure people know their work and understand all the system | 4. Ensure people know their work and their contributions to the work of the whole |

Briefly, how would you characterize connections, interactions and collaborative relationships among people and across various parts of your classroom, campus, district, or learning team?

Take a few minutes to jot down your thoughts about the **interdependence** in the system you want to explore.

HSD shows provides learners and lead learners in human systems skills and understandings to take action to influence one or more of these requisite patterns.

Deep Learning Ecology
ENVIRONMENTAL PATTERNS FOR DEEP LEARNING

DIVERSITY
1. Limit difference to focus on consistency and similarity
2. Select "allowable" diversity to conserve resources
3. Allow diversity, but don't actively pursue it
4. Ensure diversity in multiple areas, and manage resources accordingly

COHERENCE
1. Encourage individuality and self-expression without constraints of shared vision
2. Encourage separate identities, within named boundaries
3. Encourage similar identities without shaping specific decisions
4. Share vision and Simple Rules to inform decisions within a coherent whole

ADAPTIVE CAPACITY
1. Go deep in single-focus areas to ensure expertise
2. "Build the bench" by mentoring single-focus expertise
3. Train across interests and areas of expertise
4. Build systems for responsiveness in problem solving and decision making

INTERDEPENDENCE
1. Ensure efficiency by having people focus on their own work
2. Connect people between parts of the system that work together
3. Ensure people know their work and understand all the system
4. Ensure people know their work and their contributions to the work of the whole

© 2016 Human Systems Dynamics Institute. Use with permission.

Figure 3.1. Patterns that contribute to deep learning.

An Invitation to Complex Teaching and Learning

So what makes these patterns emerge?

> **So what does it look like as your patterns emerge?**

An ecology is in constant flux. Change is the constant. That change happens because tensions build within the system. As we explained earlier, an ecology (a complex adaptive system) emerges from a set of conditions:

- ▶ Open, yet bounded space
- ▶ Diverse components or participants
- ▶ Nonlinear relationships.

Under these conditions, tension builds in the differences between and among the various parts. In a human system, those tensions may build over time. When tensions build to a point that the system can't hold them anymore, energy is released, and the system re-organizes in more complex ways. Consider how you feel when faced with something you find irritating. You tolerate it, but you can feel the tension building. At some point, the tension is so strong that you take action to interrupt the irritant or to move away from its influence.

The system "self-organizes," and new, system-wide patterns emerge. Change happens. The system is transformed. New patterns of talk and action emerge from the system.

- ▶ A fight breaks out, and members of the system strike out at each other. They take sides and position themselves to engage in the battle.
- ▶ One individual experiences tension that makes it impossible to remain in the situation and walks away. Sometimes the tension is so great that the walking away is a permanent decision. Other times it might be just a cooling off period.
- ▶ The tension becomes so great that members of the system re-commit to finding a shared response.

Whatever the action, tension is released—at least for the moment.

Noticing and understanding those emerging patterns are critical to educators who try to understand what is happening in a learning ecology. Think for a moment about what we mean by "pattern." Of course, everyone knows a pattern when they see one in their living room rugs or in the clouds on a summer afternoon. In HSD, we have a more exact definition of "pattern":

> *Patterns are similarities, differences, and connections that have meaning across space and time.*

If you watch changing patterns emerge from a particular system, you can infer what might be happening there. You can interpret what you see in terms of what you know about ecologies in general—that healthy ecologies are complex systems, and the conditions that shape the complexity also generate the patterns that emerge.

Remember the conditions that define a complex system: **open boundaries, diversity,** and **nonlinear interactions**. For any complex system, its adaptive capacity depends on its ability to understand those conditions in ways that inform wise action.

Now think about those conditions in light of the essential requisites we named for creating a powerful learning ecology.

- ▶ How can you use those three conditions to leverage **diversity**?
- ▶ How can you build **coherence** as you bring together a population whose diversity is fueled by multiple perspectives and needs?
- ▶ How do you help the system build **adaptive capacity,** given differences among individuals?
- ▶ How do you build **interdependence** that allows learners to build relationships that contribute to their learning?

In a classroom system, as we mentioned above, you may see patterns of trust, risk-taking, fear, competition, and/or curiosity emerge over time. Patterns can either be positive or negative. They can either support or discourage generative learning. The patterns in you learning ecology depend on the conditions you, as the lead learner, set. HSD provides you the knowledge and skills you need to set conditions that increase the chances you will see the patterns you intend.

Patterns can arise in thoughts and actions of individuals or groups. Learners come together, and their interactions form patterns. Patterns emerge as teachers plan together. Parent-teacher relationships shape patterns across the school or school district. When a similar pattern emerges in multiple places across the system—for example, curiosity—that pattern is amplified, or made stronger. That stronger pattern can influence what happens throughout the system.

Emergent patterns like this can be seen in many aspects of the community. They combine to create an emergent and ever-changing culture. Educators often describe the culture of a classroom, a campus, or a larger community. Individuals in the system have power to notice and name these patterns. They can interpret what the patterns mean for the system. And they can set conditions that may shape or influence other patterns. In fact, that's how we can define responsive teaching:

> *Responsive teachers see, understand, and influence patterns of individual and collective learning. In the same way, responsive administrators see, understand, and influence patterns in parts of their school campus or district, as well as patterns across the whole. In fact, in deep learning ecologies, we invite students to see, understand, and influence patterns in their experiences, in their reading and writing, and in other disciplinary learning.*

An Invitation to Complex Teaching and Learning

The following table suggests ways responsive lead learners can shape a generative, sustainable learning ecology.

Table 3.1. What actions set conditions to influence patterns of deep learning ecologies?

Complex Systems → / Healthy Learning Ecologies ↓	**Open** (Complex systems are open to multiple forces and influences from internal and external sources.)	**Highly Diverse** (Complex systems bring together agents who are different from each other in multiple ways.)	**Nonlinear** (In complex systems, shared and individual histories shape current interactions, making the future unknown and unknowable.)
Diversity	Think critically about multiple influences and forces they face in the classroom and in their communities	Leverage their differences to enhance their systems in generative ways	Share and understand their own and others' pasts, in ways that contribute to generative, sustainable work
Coherence	Consider forces and influences they face to find best fit for them and for the whole system	Make choices and decisions that ensure similar responses across the system	Use past learning and shared aspirations to consider next wise actions
Adaptive Capacity	Identify strategies and understandings that enable learners to see, understand, and influence patterns that shape their worlds	Share existing individual strategies and build new strategies that leverage shared skills and abilities	Reflect on and learn from the past to work toward shared aspirations
Interdependence	Recognize the value of shared resources and perspectives in dealing with unknown and unpredictable forces	Consider others' contributions and needs, according to existing challenges and opportunities	Share past learning and build on it to approach future challenges

- ▶ What can you do, in planning your learning ecology, to explore these questions about yourself and the learners who will be joining your system?

- ▶ What can you do to support your learners in exploring these questions to enhance their individual and shared learning in the ecology?

- ▶ What would you add to add to this set of options?

Now what is your assessment of your own learning ecology?

How does all this apply in your learning ecology? Whether you are a teacher, an administrator, a librarian, a counselor, or another agent/stakeholder in your school, you can consider what you see and hear in your learning ecology. To what extent do you notice evidence of these patterns that typically emerge in healthy ecologies:

Now what is happening in your learning ecology?

- Diversity?
- Coherence?
- Adaptive Capacity?
- Interdependence?

You can use the form on the following pages to record your responses. Include as much detail as you can.

- **What?** Notice the patterns. You can use the "Requisites for a Learning Ecology" to describe what you notice in terms of each one.

- **So What?** Interpret what these patterns mean for the health of your ecology.

- **Now What?** Consider your options for action to shift these patterns—to reinforce the healthy, productive, or generative patterns and to avoid or change the less healthy patterns.

- **Now What?** What are your new questions about the challenges in your ecology?

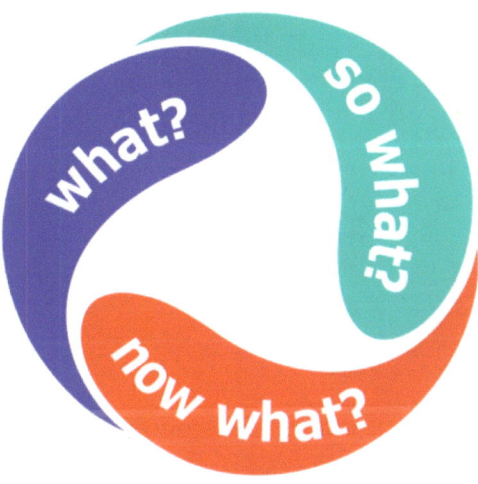

An Invitation to Complex Teaching and Learning

Assess the Health of Your Learning Ecology

Diversity

What patterns of diversity do you see?

So what do those patterns contribute to learning in your classroom?
So what do those patterns detract from learning in your classroom?

Now what can you do to shift the conditions:
- More open or more closed?
- More or less diverse?
- Built on past histories and shared learning for all learners?

Coherence

What patterns of coherence exist?

So what do those patterns contribute to learning in your classroom?
So what do those patterns detract from learning in your classroom?

Now what can you do to shift the conditions:
- Provide simple rules to ensure coherent response to system tensions?
- Amplify the similarities that exist?
- Build on past histories and shared experiences?

An Invitation to Complex Teaching and Learning

Adaptive Capacity

What patterns of adaptive capacity do you see?

So what do those patterns contribute to learning in your classroom?
So what do those patterns detract from learning in your classroom?

Now what can you do to shift the conditions:
- ▶ Help learners see and value contributions of others?
- ▶ Help learners appreciate the different contributions others bring?
- ▶ Emphasize shared interdependence for all learners?

Interdependence

What patterns of interdepence do you see?

So what do those patterns contribute to the learning in your classroom?

So what do those patterns do to detract from learning in your classroom?

Now what can you do to shift the conditions:
- More open or more closed?
- More or less diverse?
- Built on past histories and shared learning for all learners?

Part 2: Applications: Models and Methods

Module 4
Your Action: See, Understand, and Influence

Teaching is hard. No . . . that's not it. Teaching is frustrating, seemingly impossible, joyful, mind-bending, collaborative, blissful, all-consuming, and a passion. But most importantly, one thing it is NOT is static. We live in an educational world that is ever-changing because we live in a world in which people are ever-changing…our students never stop growing.
— Chris Bronke

All failure is failure to adapt, all success is successful adaptation.
— Max McKeown

Complex human systems are open to influence. They are amazingly diverse. They are connected through unpredictable, nonlinear relationships. In schools, multiple systems are layered and overlapping. They continually self-organize in surprising ways. In this environment, how do you plan? How do you take action to make a significant difference, even in the short term?

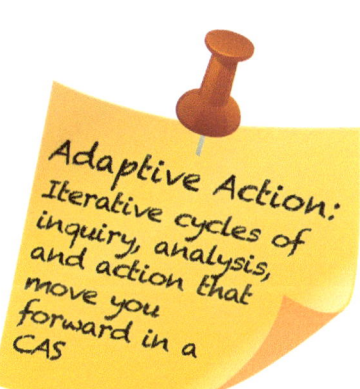

Adaptive Action: Iterative cycles of inquiry, analysis, and action that move you forward in a CAS

HSD practitioners believe that everyone in the system can influence emerging patterns if they focus on two connected practices:

- **Adaptive Action** – ongoing cycles of inquiry, reflection, and action
- **Pattern Logic** – a focus on seeing, understanding, and influencing patterns in the system

Those two practices are based on the assumption that the three conditions shape the patterns in all complex adaptive systems:

- Something holding the system together long enough for it to self-organize and generate patterns (**C**ontainers)
- Diversity within the system creates the energy for change (**D**ifferences)
- Energy and information are shared throughout the system (**E**xchanges)

Eoyang refers to these as the **CDE Model,** the conditions that shape the speed, path, and direction of self-organization.

An Invitation to Complex Teaching and Learning

In deep learning ecologies, we take action to set conditions to shape the patterns that emerge across time. This module is designed to help practitioners use Adaptive Action and Pattern Logic to set conditions to ensure healthy systems. This module is designed to help practitioners explore those three conditions and the connections among them.

What is Adaptive Action?

What kind of action planning works in complex ecologies?

As we introduced it in Module 1, Adaptive Action is an iterative inquiry cycle based on three questions: **What?**, **So What?,** and **Now What?** Asking and answering these questions can help you see, understand, and influence patterns in your systems. Engage in these ongoing cycles to find ways to adapt to changes. Continual inquiry and flexibility make your collective work more adaptable and resilient.

Since John Dewey talked about it in the early twentieth century, educators have used cycles of inquiry, reflection, and action as the foundation for responsive instruction and leadership (for example, Clay, 1991; Stringer, 2007; Wink, 2000). HSD practitioners argue that Adaptive Action is not simply recommended. It is the only effective way you can work in complex human systems. It is the preferred choice for teaching students, collegial planning, campus-wide planning, or advocating with policy makers.

In ever-changing environments, Adaptive Action is your only choice is to observe and make sense of emergent patterns. It is your tool for identifying choices and taking action to shift those patterns.

The table on the next page suggests examples of questions that students, teachers, and other people in schools might ask as they engage in Adaptive Action.

Use the sheet below to apply this tool to a particular challenge within your work. Adaptive Action can be used for system-wide issues and for long-term planning. We recommend you first focus on a relatively small challenge that involves a few people. Think in terms of a relatively short timeline.

Table 4.1. Describe your own patterns

My learning ecology: _____

What 1 or 2 patterns do I want to encourage or amplify?

▶ _____

▶ _____

What?	So What?	Now What?
▶ What am I doing? ▶ What are other people saying and doing? ▶ How do I know? ▶ What patterns do I see? ▶ What patterns do I want to see? ▶ What resources do we have? *What else?*	▶ So what does it mean that these patterns are dominant? ▶ Do we need more diversity? coherence? Adaptive Action? Interdependence? ▶ So what are my options for action? *What else?*	▶ Now what is my next wise action? ▶ Now what else do I need to know? ▶ Now what support do I need *What else?*

Record your reflections here.

An Invitation to Complex Teaching and Learning

What is Pattern Logic?

> **What does Pattern Logic help us underestand?**

When human systems change, new patterns of ideas, messages, and behavior emerge and become dominant over time. Observable patterns in these systems indicate how the system is working. You may remember that HSD defines CAS as "a collection of agents (people, groups, ideas) that interact so that system-wide patterns emerge, with the strongest patterns influencing subsequent interactions among the agents" (Dooley, 1996). Use that as a description of what you see in schools (and in life beyond schools), it makes sense that you would want to 1) observe those patterns; 2) make sense of the patterns you see; and 3) use what you see as the basis to further influence future patterns (Adaptive Action). In HSD, our reasoning that is based on this pattern-finding process is called **Pattern Logic**.

Pattern Logic: Exploration of conditions that shape speed, path, and direction of pattern emergence in self-organizing systems

Pattern Logic is the foundation of Adaptive Action. Pattern Logic is how HSD practitioners describe their arc of reasoning in Adaptive Action. It moves from 1) evidence, 2) to an analysis and interpretation of patterns 3) to a list of options for action. Pattern Logic is based on our understanding of how patterns emerge in complex adaptive systems (CAS).

Let's consider what we mean by "pattern." A pattern is comprised of *"similarities, differences, and connections that have meaning across space and time."* That definition applies to visual patterns you might see in a photograph, painting, or in the clouds on a summer afternoon. But that definition also applies to patterns of that you might hear in a teacher workroom or in parent conferences. It also applies to patterns of behavior—like those that emerge in a Kindergarten classroom or a middle school cafeteria during the lunch period. When we think about the patterns—the similarities, differences, and connections—that emerge from a system of humans over time, we sometimes call them cultural norms or cultural practices. Culture emerges from a human system as identifiable patterns of communication and action.

To study how these patterns connect to the underlying dynamics of complex systems, think in terms of three ways to look at patterns in a system.

Patterns: Similarities, differences, and connections that have meaning across space and/or time.

- ▶ What is similar? What makes this system different from its context? What bounds the space?

- ▶ What are differences that are critical inside this system?

- ▶ What connections hold parts of the system together? What are the connections that build interdependence and coherence throughout the system?

We have found it most useful to think of a pattern—not as a single word—but as a complete sentence that answers these questions.

Table 4.2: Examples of possible patterns and pattern descriptions in school contexts.

Context	Examples: Look for (and name) similarities, differences, and connections in your system	
	Words or phrases tell a bit . . .	But sentences describe the whole patterns . . .
Faculty Meetings	Talk about learning	▶ Most conversations in our faculty meetings focus on what we can do to support student learning—what works and what might not be working.
	Stand in inquiry	▶ The principal and staff are always asking questions; everyone seems to take an inquiry stance toward their practice.
Cafeteria	Good supervision	▶ Adults who supervise offer support for students, helping them have a pleasant and efficient lunch time.
	Students segregate	▶ Students choose to sit with their friends.
	Students are calm	▶ Most students are calm and courteous to one another and to the staff while they eat.
Kindergarten Classroom	Quiet entry	▶ Children typically come into the classroom in the morning in a calm way, first washing their hands and then moving to one of three learning centers.
	Independent work	▶ The teacher encourages independent learning. For example, when children come to ask the teacher for assistance with an individual task, she first asks them to explain what they have already done to solve their problems.

In Table 4.2, note single words or phrases are not wrong, but don't give enough description that the reader would know what was really happening. A fuller description contributes to the explanation you can use to shift the pattern.

We have learned it is often useful to use Pattern Logic *retrospectively*. **What** patterns have you noticed in your system in the past? Which of those patterns are influencing your work today? **So what** do those mean to various people in the system? **Now what** actions can you take to move toward deeper learning for all?

An Invitation to
Complex Teaching and Learning

We have also learned to use Pattern Logic *prospectively* as we look to the future. What patterns do you want to generate in your system? What might those patterns mean to various people? What actions might you take to generate those desired patterns?

Pattern Logic provides deeper understanding as you explore your system retrospectively, and as you set conditions for patterns you want in the future. The major portion of this book is dedicated to sharing many of those models, but there is one that offers the essence of Pattern Logic: the CDE Model.

What is the CDE Model?

> **What can I learn about conditions that shape patterns I see?**

The CDE model is based on Glenda Eoyang's research and practice over the last two decades. She has facilitated change initiatives in large and small organizations around the world (Eoyang, 2000). Her CDE model explains how three interdependent conditions influence the patterns inside that system.

You can't control or predict what happens in these systems. You can, however, use Pattern logic to identify and interpret patterns. This allows you to infer what might be influencing the system. Then you can use what you learn about those patterns as a springboard to action (Adaptive Action). Pattern Logic gives us a way to think about options for action to influence those patterns. We can amplify what we want to preserve. We can damp what is not fit for our purpose. As we look at patterns, we focus on the three foundational conditions of complex adaptive systems:

- ▶ Container – conditions that hold the system together
- ▶ Difference – the condition the generates a productive tension in the system
- ▶ Exchange – the condition that connects parts of the system, so that energy or information can flow.

Eoyang wrote the following suggestions about how to work in complex systems (http://www.hsdinstitute.org/resources/pattern-logic-blog.html). Here we see an explanation of Pattern Logic integrated with a definition of the conditions of self-organizing systems, or the CDE Model.

> **Container: Discover the boundaries that define the space.** What belongs together? What clusters of things are the same? What groups, areas, spaces are set apart in some way from others? Where are the walls, and what are the doors and windows? In Pattern Logic, we call these containers. They can be physical—like real walls or cubicles. They can also be social, political, emotional, informational. Anything in the space that divides the "same" from the "other" acts as a container in Pattern Logic.Containers are varied and massively entangled in any situation. Being conscious of containers allows you to thrive. Political acumen is the ability to create, respect, or cross boundaries, and the wisdom to choose when to do which.

Figure 4.1 represents containers within a human system. Think about the multiple boundaries or the containers in your learning ecology or system.

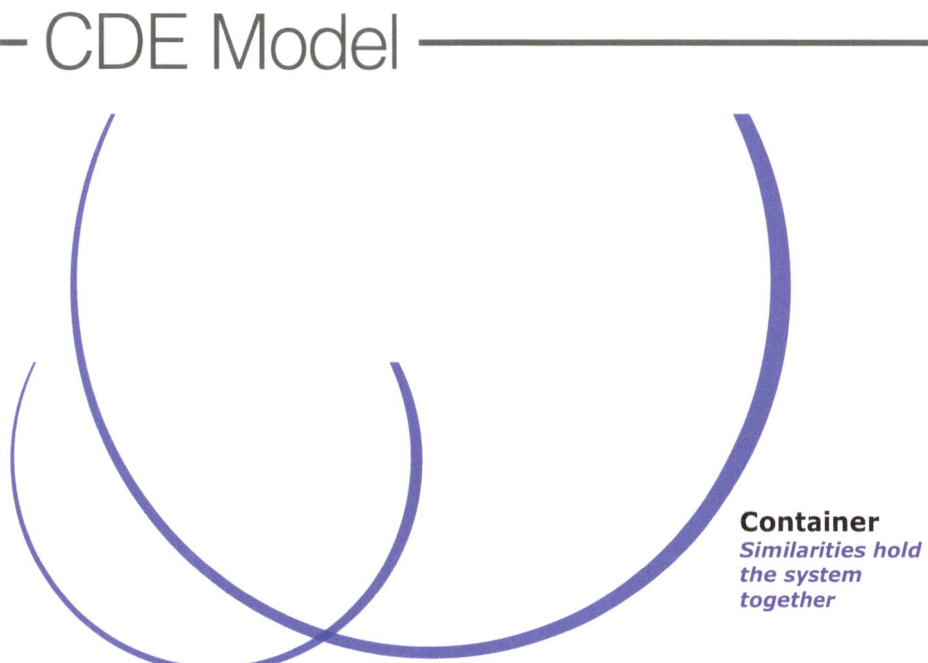

Figure 4.1. Container: one of Eoyang's three conditions of complex adaptive systems.

Difference: Find the differences that make a difference. Any human system includes more differences than you can count. On the first day of work, for example, you pay attention to language, location, colors, light, expectations, relationships, values, instructions, HR procedures, where to find the lunchroom, whether people are smiling and how loudly people speak. These and thousands of other differences inundate every minute of your first day on the job. In HSD, we refer to these system characteristics as differences.

In any new space, you don't know which differences are important, so you don't know where to focus. It can feel like you are in the middle of a west Texas sandstorm—seeing lots of things and not knowing which ones to pay attention to. As you use your Pattern Logic, you will focus on a few significant differences. They will help you see what is happening and make decisions about what to think and do.

It is important to remember that differences that make a difference change all the time. Even after you are familiar with a situation, critical differences will change without warning. In a simple example, budget might be most important when you are talking to your boss, while schedule matters to team members, and quality concerns the students' families. The significance of differences is based on context, and because contexts change all the time, so do the differences that make a difference. Pattern Logic helps you pay attention to see and respond when significant differences shift.

Figure 4.2 represents two of Eoyang's conditions of complex adaptive systems—the container and difference. Think of various differences in your ecology, or learning system. Which of those differences really matter? Learning objectives? Various perspectives or viewpoints? Demographic diversity? Cultural or linguistic differences?

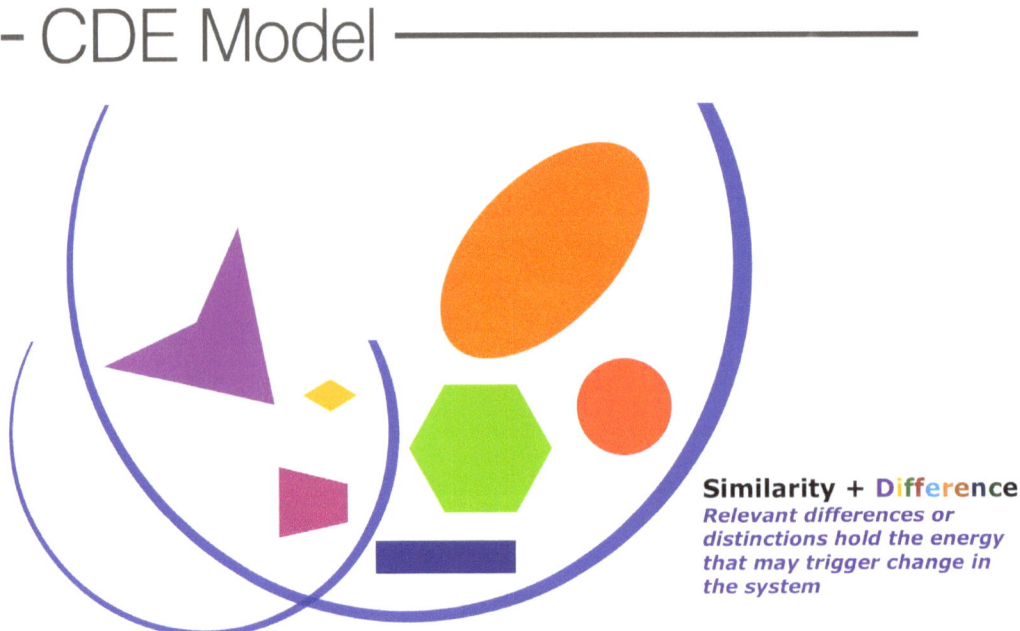

Figure 4.2. Container and Difference, two of Eoyang's conditions of complex systems.

Exchange: Explore connections between and among. People are always connected, sometimes to things or ideas and sometimes to each other. Those connections, which we call exchanges, determine when and how things change. When exchanges are tight, things change quickly. Teachers give quick feedback in clear and specific terms to support faster learning. When an annual evaluation process provides feedback that is not very specific or meaningful, that looser exchange will lead to slower change.

The sooner you see and understand the natural connections in a space, the more prepared you are to engage consciously and with intention. That is why exchanges are such a significant aspect of the adaptive capacity that comes from Pattern Logic. Like containers and differences, exchanges are many and constantly changing. Only Pattern Logic can help you recognize and engage wisely in connections that are important for you and your group. Figure 4.3 reflects connections between the differences within containers.

— CDE Model —

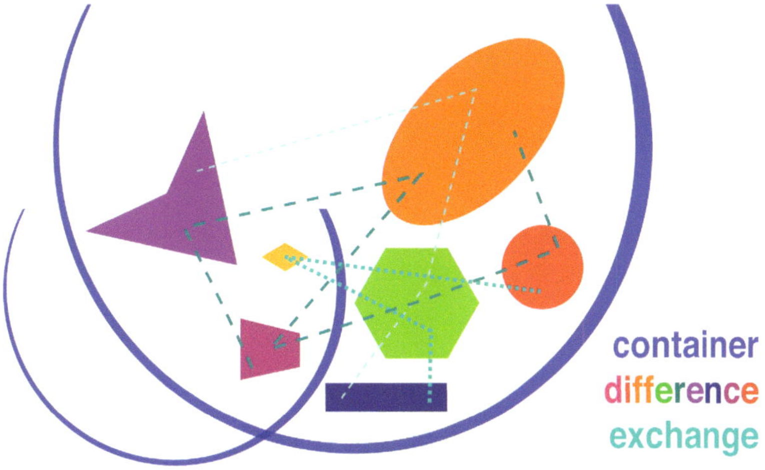

Figure 4.3. Container, difference, and exchange. Eoyang's CDE model explains conditions of complex adaptive systems

Figure 4.3 represents all Eoyang's conditions of complex adaptive systems—container, difference, and exchange. Think of exchanges in your system. How does information or energy move? Which of those potential exchanges do you emphasize? Which ones can you tweak to change the dynamics of the system?

These three conditions—containers, differences, and exchanges—shape the environment in ways that generate patterns. Table 4.3 delineates questions we might ask about each condition.

Table 4.3. Questions help reveal how conditions of a complex adaptive system shape the patterns.

The Conditions of CAS	Our questions about each condition	CDE influences on the emerging pattern
Container ▶ What holds this system together long enough for it to self-organize?	Who are we together?	**Similarities**
Difference ▶ What significant or meaningful diversities or dimensions exist in the system? ▶ Where do tensions build?	What matters most to our work?	**Differences**
Exchange ▶ What are the connections that make the spread of information or energy possible? ▶ How might we shift the tensions around the pattern?	How do we work together on what matters?	**Connections**

An Invitation to Complex Teaching and Learning

So what do we gain from CDE, PL, and AA together?

The CDE, Pattern Logic, and Adaptive Action are the keys to thriving in strange and unpredictable situations. They are the heart and soul of HSD. Our conceptual foundations, practices, models, and methods support you develop your own competence and adaptive capacity.

What generates and influence emerging patterns?	**CDE - Conditions**
So what can we learn when we analyze and interpret what we notice in our systems?	**Pattern Logic**
Now what can we use what we learn to influence the system?	**Adaptive Action**

Adaptive Action, **Pattern Logic**, and the **CDE Model** are integrated and reciprocal processes. When you engage in Adaptive Action, you use Pattern Logic to infer how conditions work together to generate patterns in your systems. You take action to "tweak" the conditions. The conditions are interdependent. When one shifts, the others shift accordingly. When one or more of the conditions shift, patterns will change. If new patterns are functional and support learning, you move forward to reinforce or amplify those patterns. If new patterns do help, you adjust in the next iteration of Adaptive Action. That is the continual inquiry/reflection/action cycle that helps you negotiate the challenges in your learning ecologies.

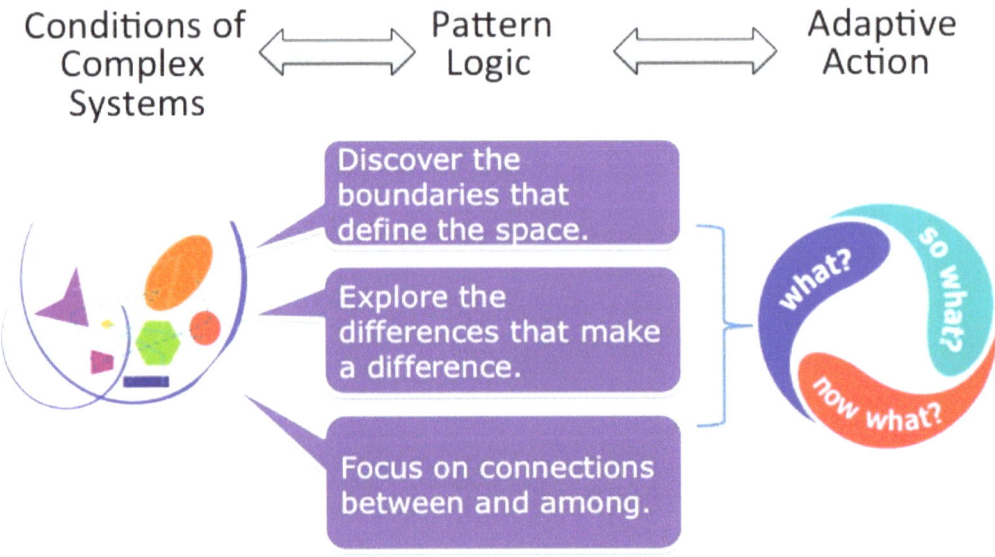

Figure 4.4. CDE, Pattern Logic, and Adaptive Action within human systems.

So what do CDE, PL, and AA mean in schools?

What do Adaptive Action, Pattern Logic, and the CDE Model look like when you use them to set conditions for a Deep Learning Ecology? The best way to respond to this question is with an example.

> **How can I use these three concepts to understand my system?**

Let's say a seventh-grade language arts teacher has noticed that her students seem unwilling to take risks as authors. The following questions suggest how that teacher might integrate Adaptive Action, Pattern Logic and the CDE Model to shift that pattern among her students. Can you point to the questions that connect to CDE? To Pattern Logic? To Adaptive Action? Can you see how these are integrated so intimately that you can't really do one of these by itself?

Together, these three methods/models help you describe, interpret, and influence the patterns in your system. You don't have to merely follow your hunches, and you don't have to blindly use trial and error. You can use these three foundational models/methods to be systematic about your decisions to influence the patterns in your learning ecologies.

Table 4.4. CDE, Pattern Logic, and Adaptive Action within human systems

What is the current pattern?	Who or what? (C)	Differences that matter? (D)	Connections? (E)
I focus on individual strengths and targets for growth through a number of classroom writing practices.	The students and I, as writers, are together in this work.	Individual strengths and targets for writing	▶ Daily writing ▶ Writing conferences ▶ Reading Mentor Texts
The boys tend to choose topics about sports; girls write about adventures with friends and family.	The girls and boys choose topics for writing.	Students have different interests and background knowledge	▶ Free choice writing ▶ Authors' chair
Although a few of the students have become enthusiastic authors, several students are reluctant to share what they have written.	All the students write and share their writing, but some reluctantly.	Extent to which students are eager and enthusiastic writers	▶ Free writing ▶ Author's chair ▶ Writer's Notebook

An Invitation to Complex Teaching and Learning

So what does the current pattern mean?	Who or what? (C)	Differences that matter? (D)	Connections? (E)
I would like to see all the students volunteering to write about a wider range of topics and to volunteer to publish their writing for their classmates.	Both girls and boys are choosing to stay in their comfort zones; not taking risks (too risky to choose an unfamiliar topic or for the three students to share their work with audiences.)	Whether or not students are volunteering to share their writing with audiences Width of the range of topics (rather than stereotypical topics)	Find more supportive and rewarding exchanges that make the feedback worth the risks.

Now what patterns do I want and what shall I do to generate them?	Who or what? (C)	Differences that matter? (D)	Connections? (E)
I would like to see all the students volunteering to share their writing about a wider range of topics.	The students and I, as writers, are together in this work.	Volunteering to share writing with audiences Width of range of topics, rather than gender stereotypical topics)	▶ Daily writing ▶ Sharing first in pairs and small groups ▶ Mentor Texts by men and women writing about non-stereotypical topics ▶ Student blogs where students post their stories and get responses for classmates

Now what?

Now what will I do to shift patterns in my classroom?

Pattern Logic helps us slow down and reflect on the patterns in our systems. Remember that a pattern is comprised of similarities, differences, and connections that have meaning across space and time. As you identify a pattern, try framing it as a whole sentence. Rather than "I see a pattern of trust in our school," try "Students and teachers clearly trust one another enough to be open about their mistakes."

Think of one system that is significant in your work. It may be a group of people (like a team of teachers) or a process (like the annual budget process). Try listing the patterns in this system. Use the chart to brainstorm for similarities (who or what), the distinctions that matter (differences), and the relevant connections (exchanges). There are no "correct" answers; the goal is to analyze the patterns so that new possibilities for action become obvious.

Table 4.5: Your Pattern Logic Analysis

Current Pattern?	Who or what? (nouns)	Differences? (modifiers)	Connections or exchanges? (verbs)

Record your observations and insights here:

Module 5
Praxis: Connect Theory and Practice

It is by exposing what we do to the light of the knowledge that science and philosophy offer that we correct and perfect ourselves. It is this that I call "thinking the practice," and it is by thinking the practice that I learn to think and to practice better.

Paulo Friere

Dreams pass into the reality of action. From the actions stems the dream again; and this interdependence produces the highest form of living.

Anais Nin

Critics of schools have long pointed to the deep and wide chasm between theory and practice. That pattern is persistent. As HSD practitioners, we ask what conditions (CDE model) deep in the system might result in this pattern?

Maybe it's about **containers**. Professional boundaries between practitioners and researchers are simply too strong to allow interactions between them.

Maybe it's about **differences**. Practitioners typically focus on differences around "what works" and researchers typically focus on differences that explain "how and why things work."

Maybe it's about **exchanges**. Researchers and practitioners often speak different languages, to different audiences.

Whatever conditions (CDE) shape the emergent pattern, it reflects a disconnection between the two groups. Too often, researchers make recommendations grounded only in theory. Practitioners often dismiss those recommendations as irrelevant to their daily work. Neither group listens to the other. Neither informs the other.

In a deep learning ecology, theory and practice are two dimensions of the same system. In HSD, we work to integrate theory and practice. Like other pragmatic approaches, HSD asserts that the best theory is practical and that the best practice is grounded in theory. In fact, rather than talking about them as separate entities, we choose to talk about "praxis." Praxis is the generative integration of theory and practice, where each informs, supports, and extends the other.

An Invitation to Complex Teaching and Learning

What is praxis?

What does it mean to blend theory and action?

We see praxis as the integration of theory (what we know and believe) with practice (what we do). Praxis refers to an essentially human drive toward creativity and free expression. It is essentially a rich and complex inquiry-reflection-action process. Freire points to praxis as "reflection and action upon the world in order to transform it" (2000). Other educational theorists and activists who use the term also remind us that praxis is more than merely theoretically-informed action. It is a deeply creative process grounded in dialogue and work toward hopeful, generative, and democratic goals (for example, Carspecken, 1996; Kemmis, 2010; Wink, 2010).

People who consciously and thoughtfully engage in praxis take a stance that includes both curiosity and humility. That calls to mind the HSD definition of inquiry we include in Module 1, represented in Figure 5.1.

Inquiry

▶ turn judgment into curiosity

▶ turn disagreement into shared exploration

▶ turn defensiveness into self-reflection

▶ turn assumptions into questions

Figure 5.1: Actions that set conditions for the pattern of inquiry in a complex adaptive system.

Here are some examples of praxis we have recently seen in PK-12 schools:

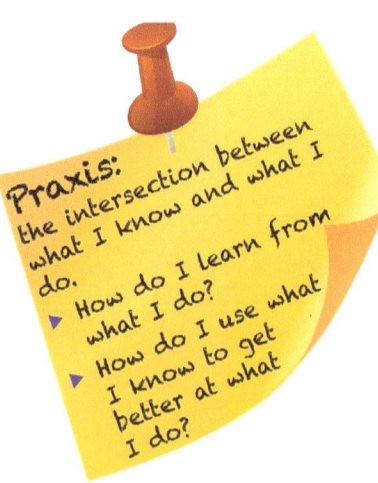

- Suzanne, a third-grade teacher takes recommendations from a professional development workshop about "Mentor Texts." She creates a lesson in which her students find their favorite sentences in their independent reading books. They write those sentences on strips of paper and cut the words apart. Then they study how, as authors, they might put the words back together in new ways.

- Jane, a high school English teacher participates in a campus Professional Learning Community focusing on instructional games. Then she works with her colleague in social studies. They "gamify" the 10th-grade English and history courses. They invite students to read, write, and discuss primary documents. As a result, students accept challenges, earn points, and score wins.

- Cindy, a campus principal, provides resources and time for all instructional staff on her campus to read professional articles and engage in action research. They have time and support to share what they learn with one another in a "teaching fair" at the end of the school year.

- Using an article they read online as a model, James and Rossana, who teach fifth grade and Kindergarten, collaborate to set up "reading and writing buddies." They pair their students, forming literacy partnerships invite both younger and older students. At both levels, the students engage in authentic reading and writing opportunities.

- Briana recently finished a master's thesis related to the maker movement. She sets up a "maker space" in her high school library. Her goal is to invite students to come into the library to design small robots in their free time. This new space increases the number of students who visit the library. Surprisingly, the numbers of books checked out increases over the last three months of the school year.

Each of these educators faced a specific challenge. They responded by finding published theory or research. They integrated this theoretical knowledge with their practical knowledge about their students and their local campus. They took action, and they watched the results.

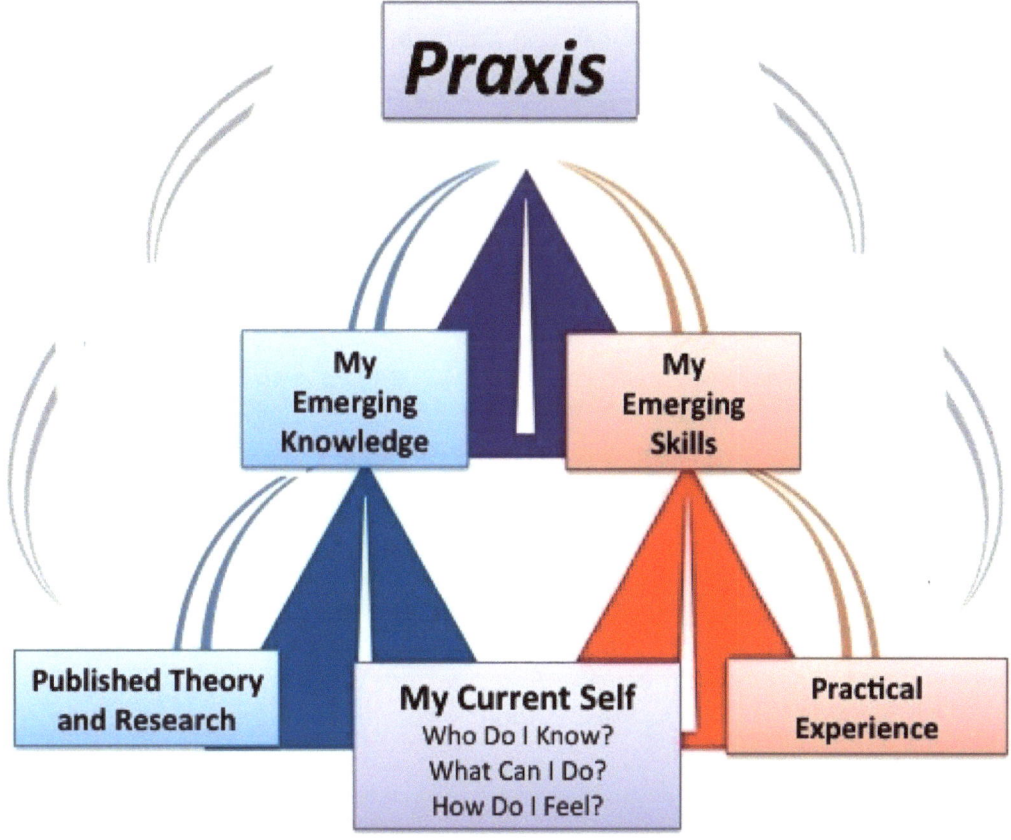

Figure 5.2: The Praxis Triangle represents the integration of theory and practice through Adaptive Action.

**An Invitation to
Complex Teaching and Learning**

Although this inquiry-reflection-action process is too complex and dynamic to be captured in a static, two-dimensional drawing, Figure 5.2 offers a partial representation of its critical features. The three triangles represent how the educator engages in inquiry, reflection, Adaptive Action, and Pattern Logic. Begin at the bottom, center of the figure. As lead learner, you bring your knowledge, skills, and attitudes to particular challenges. Through cycles of Adaptive Action (**What?** / **So What?** / **Now What?**), you search published research for possible explanations and answers to build your emerging knowledge. You engage in cycles of Adaptive Action in your practical experience. This builds your emerging skills. Your knowledge and skills are integrated in your praxis. It happens in ongoing cycles of Adaptive Action (inquiry, reflection, and action) that build your personal theory-to-practice connections.

So what integrates theory & practice in a deep learning ecology?

> **How do I blend theory and action in my classroom?**

Consider how a first-grade teacher might bring practical experiences and observational data together with recommendations from professional books to develop his emerging praxis.

Sam, a first-grade teacher, is frustrated about the progress of his student, Suzanne, who is not moving forward as a reader. After three months of instruction, although Suzanne can use the sounds of letters to pronounce unfamiliar words, her oral reading is still very halting. Her comprehension is not improving as quickly as her classmates'. Rather than referring Suzanne to the reading specialist down the hall, Sam considers Suzanne and her reading progress. He is looking for patterns that can help him think of what to do next.

What?

Each day for two weeks, Sam makes time to listen to Suzanne read, systematically recording and analyzing the oral reading. He asks her to do quick retelling to determine what she is focusing on as she reads. He also refers to a book from his graduate course to see what the experts say about this reader's strengths and instructional targets.

So What?

Sam decides that Suzanne is focusing primarily on the letter-sound puzzle. She doesn't understand that the whole story is supposed to fit together to make sense. She seems to be focusing on sounding out words at the expense of following the meaning of the story. She does not seem to be using the pictures, or even her background knowledge about what is happening in the story.

Now What?

Sam decides to have more conversations with his class (including Suzanne) about using the pictures and their background knowledge, along with the letters and sounds, to figure out what the whole story might mean. Based on one of the articles he read, he decided to talk to his students about how they need to become "Reading Detectives" (Goodman, 1999).

This process convinces Sam that he has been focusing his instruction on sound-symbol correspondence because that's what the mandated instructional program emphasizes. This reading and reflection on the students' data is shifting his understandings about how people make sense of text. He begins to balance his instructional strategies with his young readers. He vows to watch his students more carefully to see what cues they use as they read and retell their stories. He is curious about what he might learn about this from watching his students' journal writing.

Refer to the Praxis Triangle to see how it represents Sam's work. He used published resources—the graduate textbook—to develop emerging understanding about what is happening and why. He gathered more data from his practical experiences about students' reading accuracy and comprehension. This built his skill-based, practical understandings. Through reflection, he integrated his emerging knowledge and skills about how his students make sense of their reading. This dynamic use of Adaptive Action to integrate knowledge and practice led him to decide on particular instructional actions and to new questions. This is praxis—the integration of knowledge making and knowledge using.

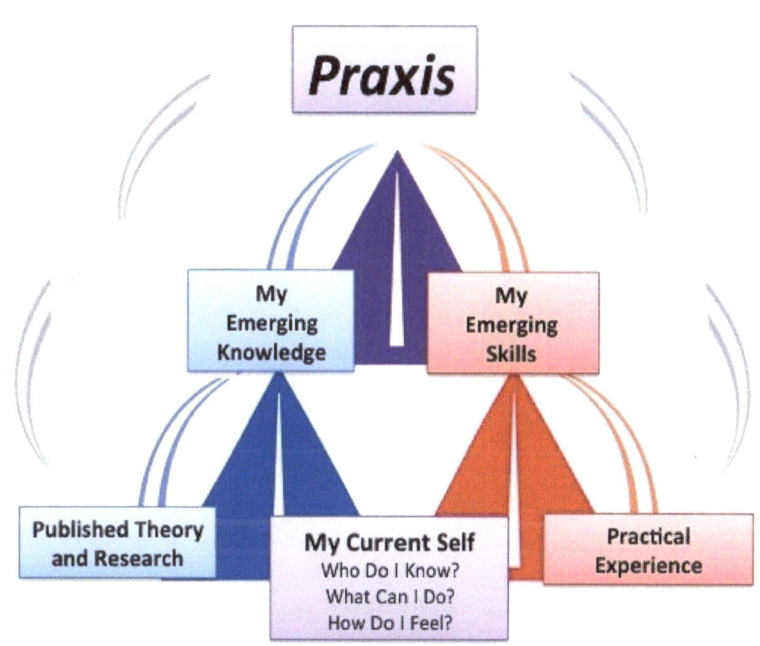

As an effective and responsive teacher, he continually engages in praxis. He uses creative inquiry and reflection to integrate his theoretical understandings with practice. This process leads him to wise action. He learns from what is happening in the classroom. He gathers insights from published research and theory. He brings those together in his praxis to make decisions about his next teaching action.

Now what is your Praxis Triangle?

Use Figure 5.2 to apply the Praxis Triangle to your work. How accurately does it represent your professional learning and your professional action?

You can use it to analyze a past experience. Name a challenge you faced. Ask yourself:

Now how does my practice fit the Praxis Triangle?

- How did I find theoretical information to guide my decisions?
- How did I analyze my practical experiences to inform my next best action?
- How did I integrate theoretical insights and practical knowledge to evaluate instructional options? What were benefits and potential pitfalls of each?

Or use the Praxis Triangle to plan for future use of Adaptive Action and Pattern Logic.

- Develop a plan to explore related research and theory
- Gather data and make sense of your practical experiences.

To support your praxis, you may want to

- Use a teaching journal
- Meet with colleagues in a professional learning community
- Gather student work and anecdotal records
- Schedule time in your work week for quiet reflection time.

Educators in all roles use these tools and structures to support praxis. On the other hand, educators' generative inquiry and creative decisions may be limited by:

- Curricular mandates
- Scripted instructional programs
- Budget constraints
- High stakes accountability systems

When that happens, educators struggle to engage praxis to establish deep learning ecologies.

Use the form on the next page to explore application of theory in a particular challenge you see.

YOUR TURN

Think of a particular challenge you face in your system, and reflect on your praxis.

1. What is a significant challenge you face? List significant features of that challenge, including patterns of decision making and action you see in the system around you (refer to module 4).

2. What does practical experience tell you about this challenge?

3. What do theory and research tell you about this challenge?

4. How do your emerging theory and practice combine to suggest possible actions?

Module 6
Connect: Generative Engagements

A choir is made up of many voices, including yours and mine. If one by one all go silent, then all that will be left are the soloists. Don't let a loud few determine the nature of the sound. It makes for poor harmony and diminishes the song.
Vera Nazarian

When people don't express themselves, they die one piece at a time.
Laurie Halse Anderson

In the long history of humankind (and animal kind too) those who learned to collaborate and improvise most effectively have prevailed.
Charles Darwin

A teacher who establishes rapport with the taught, becomes one with them, learns more from them than he teaches them.
Mahatma Gandhi

In deep learning ecologies, relationships and dialogue between and among teachers and learners are the heart of the matter. Educators often cite the saying that "People don't care how much you know until they know how much you care." But caring is not enough. How does caring lead to wise action? Just as a rainforest needs certain conditions to sustain itself, a learning community needs particular conditions to sustain the patterns that support deep learning. We talk about those as generative engagements.

What are Generative Engagements?

Generative engagements are interactions that allow people in a system to create something new and different. They are patterns of interaction and collaboration that allow each individual to participate fully, contributing where possible. They are patterns where individuals accept others' contributions. People share challenges and gifts to ensure a fair and just system.

> **What makes engagements more or less generative?**

Generative Engagement is based on assumption that each individual brings a unique mix of experiences and perspectives. Learners come from different homes. Each brings a distinct personality, experience, and cultural knowledge. Each child brings unique patterns of behavior. Besides individual differences, people become who they are because of historical, socio-economic, cultural/political dynamics in larger systems. Differences in power and status also contribute to patterns.

Generative Engagement: interactions and connections that allow people to come together to create something new and different

Over time, lack of collaboration has been seen as a major challenge to successful school change. Limited time in the work day is certainly a factor that limits collaboration. At the same time, deep, productive collaboration takes a special skill. It requires people to work together across their differences. Much of the current literature about diversity and collaboration speaks to differences on a larger scale (subject area, role, experiences, for instance). In HSD we recognize that more subtle differences (opinions, perspectives, experiences) can also create conflict and misunderstanding in systems. These subtle differences can also limit collaboration.

In schools, people often don't know how to negotiate significant differences so they can collaborate well. In human systems dynamics terms, they don't know how to set conditions for their system to self-organize into patterns of collaboration.

▶ People tend to build partnerships **(containers)** with people with whom they identify. This isolates them from others who may offer different perspectives and information.

▶ They tend to focus on **differences** that cannot be changed, rather than ones that can be negotiated.

▶ Interactions **(exchanges)** are often unconsciously exclusionary, biased, or even bigoted, as they reinforce similarities and discount/punish difference.

Those kinds of interactions limit a system's ability to accommodate difference or support collaboration. In turn, this reduces coherence and endangers sustainability across the whole. The system can become fractured and fragile.

In HSD, we believe that understanding dynamics of these emergent patterns can help us think about how to influence generative patterns. Using the CDE model (Module 4), we consider conditions for self-organization that might trigger responsive and generative relationships.

This insightful teacher tells a story that serves to illustrate the tension that can build in these differences. It also shows how tension can sometimes be released in generative ways:

> We were reading an Eve Bunting story called Flyaway Home. The kid in the book is homeless, and he feels "vulnerable," and we were talking about what it means to be "vulnerable." I have one student who's famous for going "I

don't know" whenever I ask him questions. We were talking about what "I don't know" means. I said that I think it means . . . "you're afraid to say something so you put up this shield of 'I don't know.' Instead of telling me what you don't know, tell me what you do know." And he says, "There is something I do know." I said, "What do you know?" And he says, "I feel vulnerable. " And that absolutely broke the tension, the conflict that I felt with him. Because then it became a matter of, "Well, let's talk about how that feels. I've felt that way, too. What does that mean? What do you feel vulnerable about?"

Fifth-grade teacher

This is a generative engagement. It is an exchange among people who, in that moment, enjoy equal influence (in spite of their different roles). They sincerely stand in inquiry about what the other is feeling and thinking. And they are ready to move forward together. Once this student and teacher stepped into this generative space, they were able to work collaboratively to understand this story and connect it to their lives.

So what conditions shape Generative Engagements?

As a leader in deep learning ecologies, you want to set conditions to encourage people to work together to build system resilience and sustainability. In other words, you want to set conditions for generative engagement. Those conditions will shape patterns

> **So what shapes patterns of generative engagement?**

that help the system move toward fitness and coherence. Over years of working with people in different social contexts, focus on three particular patterns. These are generative patterns we want to create and sustain: reciprocity; authenticity; and justice.

- ▶ Generative engagements require that people contribute what they can. They also allow individuals to build on one other's strengths. We call that larger pattern ***reciprocity***.

- ▶ Generative engagements let people know they are respected and honored for their unique contributions and challenges. People are able to bring their reality into the relationship. They can be themselves. We call that pattern ***authenticity***.

- ▶ Generative engagements ensure that the needs and abilities of individuals and groups are considered in the context of the whole, ensuring equal access to all resources of the system. We call that pattern ***justice***.

All three of these patterns contribute to Generative Engagement. In a collaborative relationship, people give and take in a **reciprocal** manner. They rely on each other as they collaborate on a shared task. Deep collaboration calls for each individual to bring his or her **authentic** self. Each is respected for contributing. Finally full collaboration relies on each participant being treated in a **just** manner, according to what is needed and what can be given.

Figure 6.1. Generative Engagement: Conditions for patterns of reciprocity, authenticity, and justice.

We use the CDE model (Modules 4 and 7) to name conditions that we believe will generate these patterns (Figure 6.1).

- ▶ **Container:** Shared Identity names the container that binds us together.

- ▶ **Difference:** Shared Power refers to the ability to influence and willingness to be influenced, a difference that matters in any generative relationship.

- ▶ **Exchange:** Granting and generating voice for everyone describes exchanges that contribute to generative engagement.

In the Generative Engagement model, we use the CDE configuration to show conditions that can enable individuals and groups to negotiate across their differences to work together collaboratively.

Shared Identity

Identity is how you name your similarity as you stand in a relationship. You may have shared values and beliefs that make it easy to stand together. On the other hand you may have vastly different values and beliefs. If you are to create generative engagements, you must find some common ground where you stand together.

- Who are you as fellow learners in this classroom?
- Who are you together on this campus?
- What is your relationship to one another as you work together to build a functional, productive school system?

Figure 6.2. Shared identity is about who we can be together.

These questions call you to a **shared identity**. You share who you are together. You share your work toward common goals.

Shared identity does not ask you to ignore your own identity or personality. You can retain your individuality in your relationships, as you stand in shared space to take on a task together. You identify together around ideas and principles; you share geographical location; or you care about shared affinities. To be in a generative relationship requires that you share significant issues like direction and goals. The more strongly you share a common identity, the more generative your relationship will be.

In a classroom, the goal is for the teacher and students to work in a shared relationship of teaching and learning focused on the class's common goals. Each is a unique person. In generative engagements, they come together in mutual support. The same is true of the different roles taken on at the building level or district office. And it's true among the board of directors or even with the community. Individual assets are honored within the context of an explicitly shared identity. It results in a sense of coherence that was not possible before. When people share identity, they contribute their assets to the good of the whole, and they appreciate assets others bring.

On the other hand, teacher and students can see themselves as separate and isolated as they occupy the same space. They establish a working dynamic that is more like the parallel play of toddlers. They are in the same space, playing in their own separate agendas. Sometimes they can even share their toys. But they never really having meaningful interaction, except when one has something the other wants. And in that moment, they are in conflict.

In such a relationship, there is no attention to assets. The children only look to each other to consider what one has that the other can use as his or her own. In contrast, generative engagement means that the two can come together in collaboration to share resources and perspectives. They are unified in their shared identity.

An Invitation to Complex Teaching and Learning

Shared Power

What matters to us? What do we want to influence? The Generative Engagement model defines power as, "the ability to influence."

- Who has power to influence, and who doesn't?
- How is the ability to influence assigned or earned?
- Is influence among and between members of the system balanced across time or space?
- Are the expressions and symbols of influence explicit or unspoken?

Shared power is about working together. Each person respects and accepts others' assets in balanced, equitable collaboration. There may be differences in authority or role, but those differences do not interfere with their listening to each other. The differences do not limit their mutual influence.

The issue of power focuses on what is most important in creating a generative relationship. When one person has and uses power **over** others, there is no invitation, no path for reciprocal influence. Those who engage in a generative relationship take special care with power dynamics between them:

- They listen to each other with a willingness to learn from the other.
- They intentionally put aside bias and prejudice that prevent them from considering other's assets.
- Their decisions consider the wants, needs, and/or assets. They don't make decisions based on what they think the other should want or need.

That's what we mean when we say power is balanced. Each player comes to a relationship with as much willingness to be influenced as to influence. They share power to collaborate without giving up responsibility or accountability for the work they have to do. In your working relationship with your students, you are still the teacher. But you talk with your learners about what their interests are. You attend to gathering their input. And when you can't do what they want, you let them know why. You let them know how their input was considered. You let them know why it was not acted on.

Figure 6.3. Shared power is about how we influence each other.

The same is true in "boss" and "employee" **generative relationships**. Teachers and principals have different roles. The overall accountability for the school rests on the principal's desk. When a decision is to be made, the principal gathers input from those who are to be touched by that decision. The input may be gathered directly (talking to each person) or indirectly (talking to representatives). Gathered input is considered in making the decision. Then in sharing that decision, the principal makes sure people understand how the input was used and how it influenced the decision.

Sometimes certain people in a system are assigned influence and do not allow others any level of influence. We say that in that system, power is "out of balance." Such conditions are often set and maintained through unspoken systems of privilege and entitlement. The dominant culture has the power to shape events, expectations, and rules in ways that limit the power of others. Sometimes this is labeled "systemic bias."

When one race is privileged over others, we sometimes point to "institutional racism." When this imbalance is unconscious and/or unintentional, it's referred to as dysconscious racism (King, 1991). The potential of the whole is reduced because the talents and assets of some are unavailable to the whole. Real collaboration is impossible.

On the other hand, shared power and influence expand and enhance the adaptive capacity of a system. When power is shared in a classroom, teacher and students engage together in joint inquiry. They build on each other's' assets to change or influence the disposition of the whole. As we have already stated, shared power does not ask anyone to give up authority or accountability. In a classroom where power is shared, the teacher remains the "decider" about what is studied and resources that are used. The teacher retains the role of responsibility and accountability to set the conditions for deep learning. Shared power asks that those who are decision makers share power by allowing themselves to be influenced by those who are affected by the decisions. It sets conditions for leadership and collaboration to emerge wherever it is needed across the system.

Shared Voice

How do we connect? People cannot create generative engagements unless they grant and generate voice in their relationships. Voice, in this sense, indicates individual or shared agency. It is the essence of who you are and how you express your identity as you engage with others. These engagements manifest as you speak and listen, act and observe, give and receive.

Figure 6.4. Shared voice is about granting and generating voice.

When you grant voice, you listen to others to hear their meaning; you observe without bias; and you receive graciously. When you generate voice, you speak so others can hear and understand what you say; you at in ways that allow others to perceive your meaning; and you give in ways that are timely and considerate. Generative engagements require you to be vigilant to grant and generate ovice simultaneously.

An Invitation to Complex Teaching and Learning

This can only be done when you pay attention to others' assets and needs.

In every exchange, granting and generating voice means that you make decisions about how you express yourself—verbally and nonverbally. It is about how you see or hear others. It means that you give and you take. You speak and you listen. It also means that you stand in inquiry as you seek coherence with those around you.

Non-generative Patterns of Engagement

One way to explore generative engagement is to think about what it is not. It is not distrust, fear, or lack of respect, for example. Teachers and learners often generate these non-collaborative patterns of interaction. That usually happens when they operate on familiar, comfortable preconceptions or biases. It happens when they ignore new information.

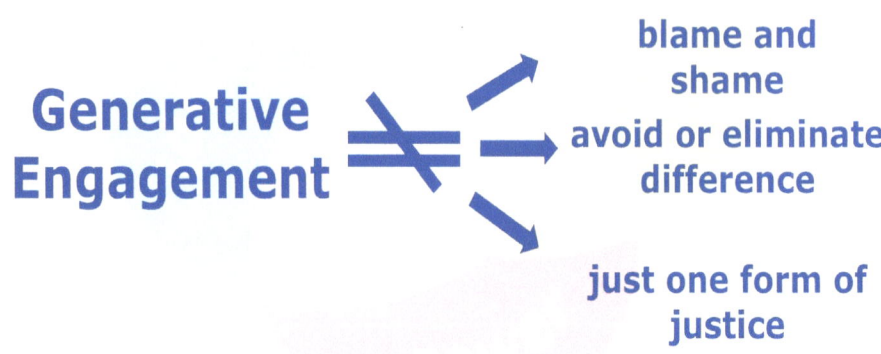

Bias robs individuals of voice, and it is often insidious. Without being aware of it, a group of people can be dominated by patterns of expectations. They tacitly agree about what is acceptable. The do not make decisions based in first-hand experiences of what works or not. Individuals can also be dominated by tradition and culture. Given the ways patterns get set in a complex adaptive system (CAS), it's easy to see how these patterns then influence the culture of the system. Some people are excluded; others are included. Individuals are judged, not by their assets, but by the expectations others have about them. Usually these patterns emerge, not because people intend to set those conditions, but because historical constraints and expectations in the system shape those patterns.

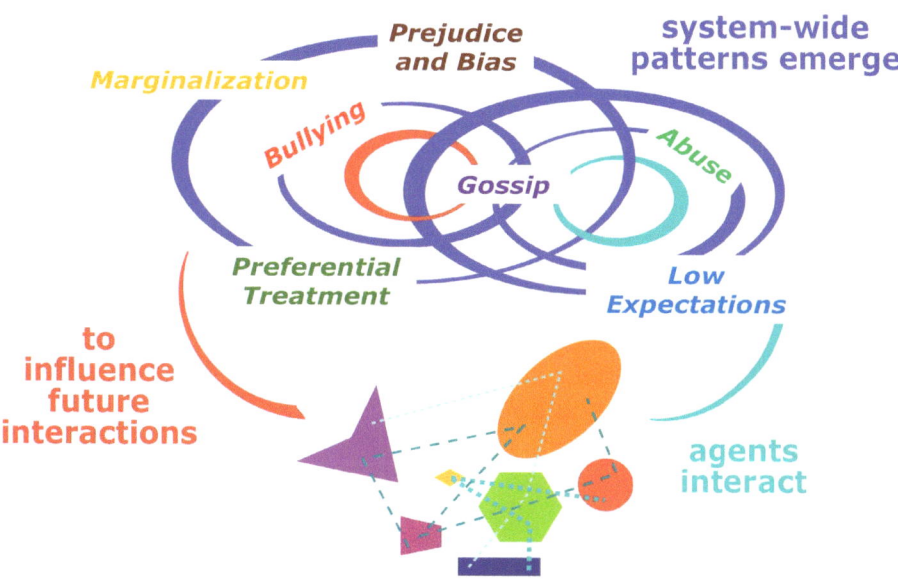

Figure 6.5. Non-generative patterns emerge in systems where agents do not share identity, power, or voice.

Think about the non-generative behaviors that emerge at all scales in a system and in multiple ways. Consider that they emerge from blatant and intentional attacks on other's rights. They also emerge from our unintended and damaging ways we interact based on our cultural biases.

- Bullying
- Abuse of authority
- Prejudice and bias
- Preferential treatment
- Gossip
- Low expectations
- Marginalization
- Inconsistency and blame

Reflect about how these behaviors limit adaptive capacity. Consider how they devalue individual assets and contributions. On the other hand, consider the potential that can be realized through engagements that don't reflect these constraints.

Generative engagement is not about avoiding or eliminating difference. Individuals make choices in every moment to move toward or away from generative engagements. There is no ultimate place where there will no longer be challenges around the differences in human systems. This model is about the choices you make each moment. It's about how you learn to work with the differences. It's about how you seek to reduce or accommodate the potential for tension in your systems.

73

An Invitation to Complex Teaching and Learning

Generative engagement is not about shame or blame. Generative engagements are about responding to differences to create the greatest "fit" across the whole system. If you can talk about generative engagement as a way of life, then people begin to see the subtler forms it takes. They have named specifically what they want, and now can build the skills to do that. They don't have to feel blamed about what they didn't see previously.

Generative engagement is not just about one form of justice like race, gender, or class. It is about how all people treat each other in each moment. It is about how they value assets in others. It is about how they work together for system sustainability.

Bullying and exploitation result from the abuse of power. Generative engagements, in contrast, seek shared power based on individual and group strength and influence. Where prejudice and bias promote one-size-fits-all answers or expectations, generative engagements create responsive, differentiated expectations for people to work together effectively. Generative engagement encourages and celebrates the multiple and diverse voices that contribute equally to coherence in the system. Fear and intolerance create separation and exclusion of individuals and groups. Generative engagements create safety and opportunities for people to express how they are different from the norm in a group.

Generative Engagements for Adaptive Capacity

Adaptive capacity and generative engagement go hand in hand. Adaptive capacity is the flexibility and responsiveness needed for collaboration (see Module 10 for more detail about adaptive capacity). Generative engagements build capacity across the system. It works well for interpersonal relationships. And it works well in a classroom or across a campus. People can talk with first graders about generative engagements. They can talk with high school seniors about creating generative engagements. It can create a common language about reciprocity, authenticity, and justice across the whole system.

This model of Generative Engagement helps us build adaptive capacity because it addresses each of the questions related to setting conditions for generative patterns.

▶ Containers: What do I do to build shared identity or to amplify those identities we share?

▶ Differences: How do I share power? How do I allow myself to be influenced by others, and how do I influence others without coercion or threat?

▶ Exchanges: How do I set up interactions to let me hear what others are saying and express myself so that they hear me?

This model is about knowing how to take action in each moment to form generative engagements. The best news is that improving system-wide collaboration and adaptive capacity does not take a huge intervention. Shifting one of those three conditions (C, D, or E) will impact the other two. For instance, when you shift your identity to align with others, you hear requests for help and input in a different way. You are more likely to be influenced by others. At the same time, if you grant others voice, you really listen to what others are saying through their words or actions. You cannot help but know more about them. You are more likely to be influenced in some way by what they say. Any one of these shifts in your behavior contributes to deeper understanding and opens the door to more powerful collaboration.

When exchanges across a system become generative, it becomes more sensitive. It is better able to sense and detect changes, challenges, and opportunities. When generative engagements are the norm in a system, it is more likely to use the broadest range of assets and contributions. It is more likely to respond in productive and sustainable ways. Generative engagements increase the points of contact among people. This creates the potential for stronger, more robust collaboration. Generative engagements increase adaptive capacity across the whole system.

Now what do you see in the Generative Engagements Model?

The Generative Engagement model can help you look back, to reflect on previous relationships. It can also help you look forward to gather insights in your planning. To do that, we suggest a modification of the "Peak Experience Activity" by the Ball Foundation.

> **Now what can I do to understand and create generative engagements?**

1. Think of a powerful collaborative experience in your professional life. Picture a time when you think everyone involved was most engaged and valued. Recall one story of this exceptional experience. Make notes about your story.

2. Find a partner and tell your story. What happened? Who was there? How did they interact? What were outcomes? How did participants feel about the experience?

3. Next, look for patterns. Each person should briefly share the highlights of his or her partner's story. Give each person 2-3 minutes. Listen for the patterns that point to Generative Engagement: authenticity; reciprocity; and justice. Use Figure 6.7 to identify the evidence for each pattern

4. Continue the conversation with your group. Reflect on actions one or more people may have taken to set conditions for these patterns. Use Figure 6.8 to track your thoughts.

    ▶ What did you or others do to build or amplify shared identities?

    ▶ What did you or others do to share power, to level both formal and informal power differences?

    ▶ What did you or others do to give opportunities for everyone to voice their perspectives and for everyone to listen to multiple perspectives?

An Invitation to Complex Teaching and Learning

Consider for yourself what you have learned in this Module and how you can continue or begin to establish generative engagements in your life.

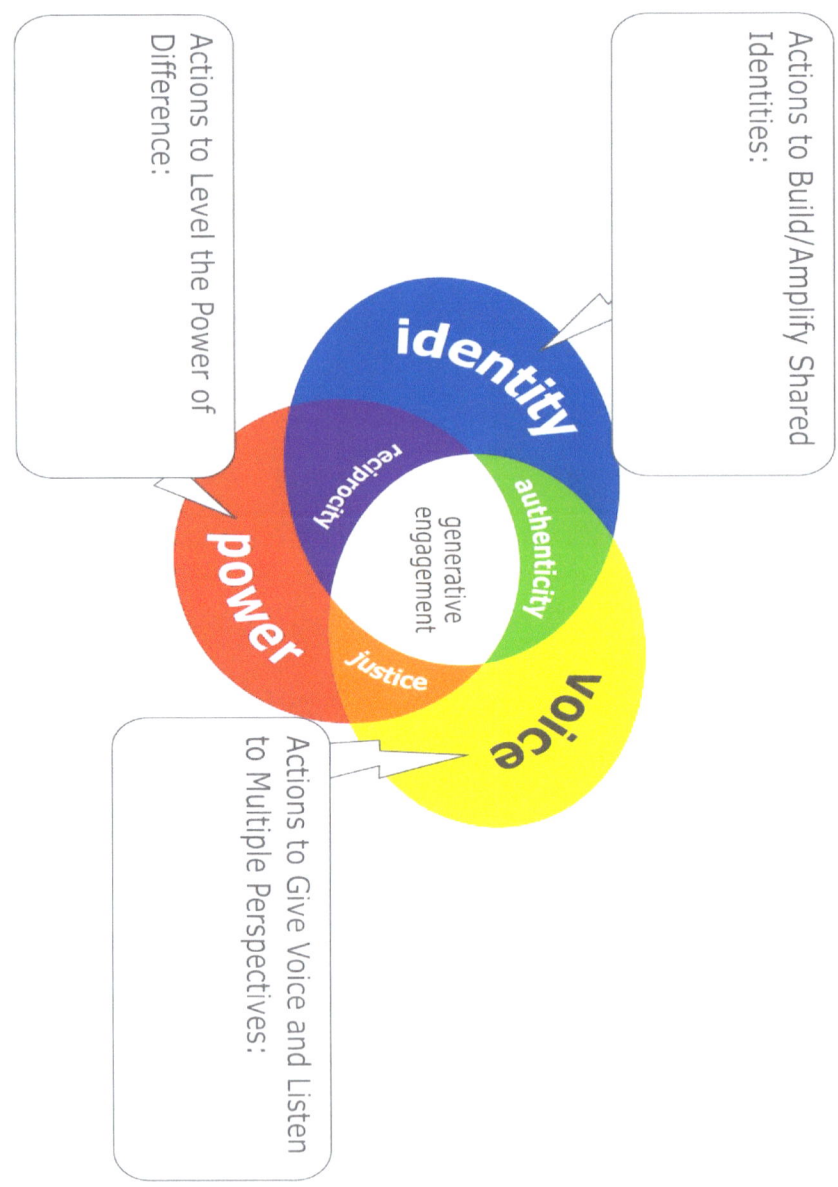

Actions to Build/Amplify Shared Identities:

Actions to Level the Power of Difference:

Actions to Give Voice and Listen to Multiple Perspectives:

Module 7
Act: Set Conditions

The important thing is not to stop questioning. Curiosity has its own reason for existing.
— *Albert Einstein*

Embracing the spirit of inquiry must begin with the belief that one can be an inquirer, a knower, an active agent in making knowledge.
— *Bruce Ballenger*

Educators can't make learning happen. But they can:

- Build relationships
- Encourage learners to take risks
- Provide materials and tasks
- Have conversations that support learning.

In other words, they can "set conditions" for generative learning. Then they watch the patterns emerge. They can take action to amplify positive learning patterns and discourage less positive patterns.

The central question for school leaders is this: How do we set conditions that build and sustain a deep learning ecology? This question leads, not to a quick fix, but to an ongoing inquiry process. In this module, we suggest "Four Big Questions" that help educators set conditions for a deep learning ecology:

- Who are we together?
- What is our learning focus?
- What differences or distinctions matter in this learning focus?
- What are our shared inquiry and reflection practices?

What conditions can we set?

What conditions shape deep learning ecologies?

HSD practitioners look below the obvious—beyond the behaviors of people in the system to its underlying dynamics. We focus on Eoyang's three "conditions of self-organizing systems" (Eoyang, 2000; Eoyang & Holladay, 2013) (Module 4). Together, these three interdependent conditions influence the path, the speed, and the direction of self-organization (Eoyang, 2000).

An Invitation to Complex Teaching and Learning

These conditions include:

- ▶ Similarities or containers *(shared identity and shared focus)*
- ▶ Differences that matter in this system *(relevant distinctions)*
- ▶ Connections or exchanges among people, ideas, documents, objects, and institutions *(shared practices)*.

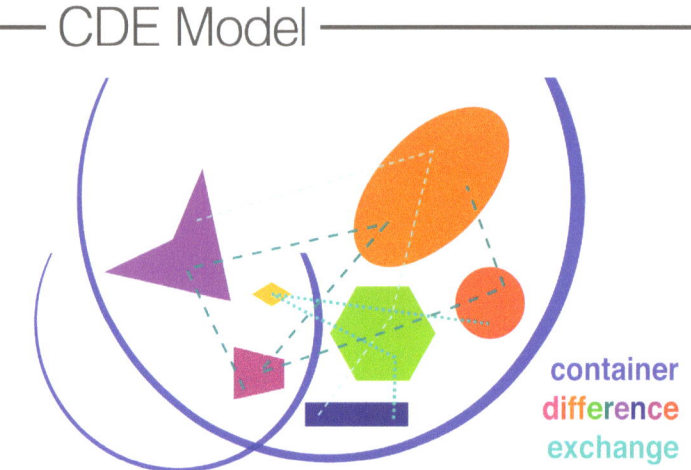

Figure 7.1. Conditions for self-organization in a Complex Adaptive System (CAS)

Anyone in the system can take action to shift one or more of these conditions to influence the speed or direction of the changing patterns in the system. See Figure 7.2 to consider ways people can influence each condition. For example:

- ▶ In the container of the classroom, teachers may choose a narrow or wide focus. For example, they may choose to work with individual students, with small groups, or with the whole class. Those flexible grouping options can influence how individual and collective learning patterns emerge.

- ▶ In considering terms of relevant differences, teachers focus on a few or many differences. For example, an English teacher can grade an essay focusing only on the ideas, not the mechanics or organizational structure—one difference instead of many.

- ▶ When shifting exchanges, teachers can send a monthly newsletter home to parents. They might send weekly e-mails to students and parents together. They can also make daily posts to the class page on Facebook. They can use all three, along with myriad others, to share information.

Each of the decisions referenced can influence one or more of the conditions. Teachers make decisions about how to do that. Their decisions increase the chances they can influence the dynamics of the system and influence patterns that ultimately emerge.

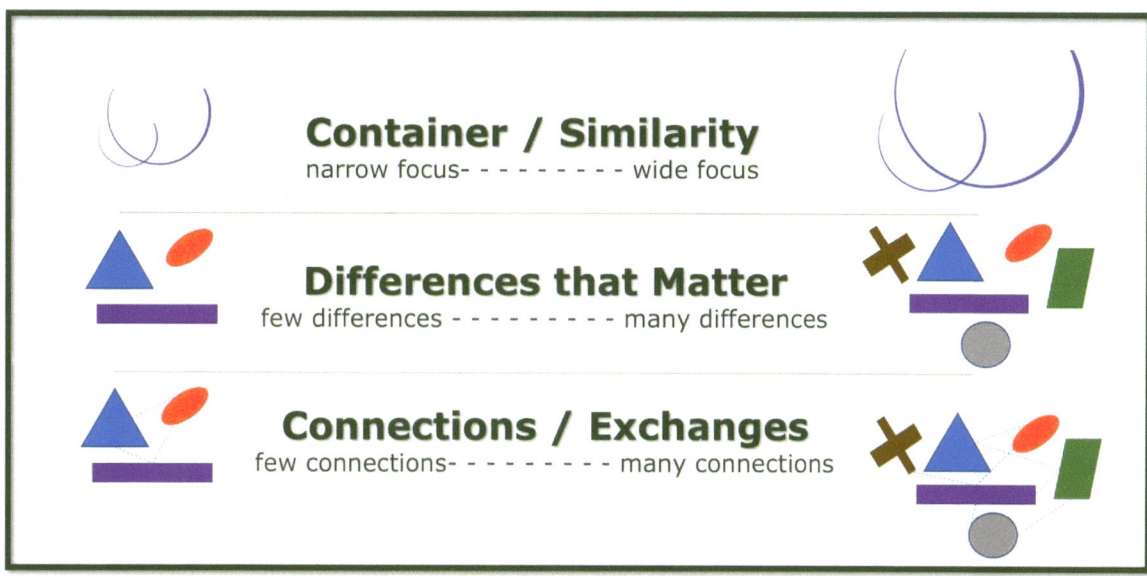

Figure 7.2. Range of options can shift conditions of self-organizing dynamics.

Notice that these three conditions are interdependent. For example, if you narrow the focus (smaller container), you will automatically be including fewer differences. If you increase the number of exchanges, you will probably also introduce more difference into the system. When you change one, the others will shift in unpredictable ways. That's why you deliberately engage in Adaptive Action and Pattern Logic. You observe and interpret existing patterns and their underlying conditions. Then you take the next best step to shift conditions. This approach is never "one and done." It's an ongoing process. You take one step; then you watch the patterns shift before you decide what your next step should be. It's an iterative process where what is learned in one cycle can be used to inform actions in later cycles.

We have found that some educators are interested in these detailed explanations of how the complex dynamics work, but many educators are less interested in the underlying dynamics and more curious about tools to use in their daily work. The "Four Big Questions" we referenced at the beginning of this module is a useful tool, whether or not the lead learner is interested in considering the shifting conditions in his or her learning ecology.

So what are the Four Big Questions for learning ecologies?

Consider what holds a learning ecology together are its similarities. Know that what generates tension and energy are the differences that exist. Remember that connections allow information and energy to flow through the system. You use the four questions stated at the beginning of this module to set these conditions for generative learning dynamics.

What 4 Questions clarify conditions for a deep learning ecology?

The table below explains how this tool fits the underlying conditions of learning ecologies. As learners and lead learners ask and answer the "Four Big Questions (in

An Invitation to Complex Teaching and Learning

the third column), they make important decisions about how to set conditions for generative learning.

Table 7.1. Guiding questions set conditions for a deep learning ecology.

Underlying Condition	Features of a Learning Ecology	Guiding Questions to Set Conditions in a Deep Learning Ecology
Similarities	Shared Identity	Who are we as a learning team/class?
	Shared Learning Focus	What are we learning about?
Differences	Relevant Distinctions	Which differences or distinctions are relevant to our learning focus?
Exchanges	Shared Practices	What shared practices emphasize Pattern Logic and Adaptive Action?

By asking and answering these questions, you can set conditions for generative learning patterns to emerge because each of these questions focuses on a feature of the system's self-organizing dynamics. In other words, each of these questions focuses on one aspect of the system that can fundamentally influence learning. Let's consider each of these questions more closely.

Shared Identity

Who are we together? The best teachers you know spend significant time and energy beginning each school year by building relationships among their students. The best principals you know work to build collegial relationships among staff members. These gifted individuals know the importance of belonging to a group with a shared focus. This insight is not original with us, of course. For example, years ago, Frank Smith recommended that all language arts teachers build a "literacy club" in their classrooms. He encouraged them to make sure that every child was a full-fledged member of that club (1987). That's about shared identity—a shared understanding about who we are as a learning team.

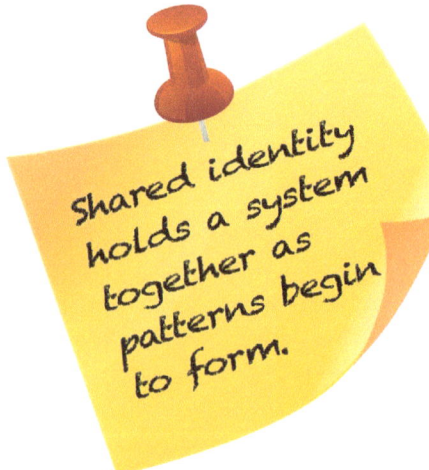

At the campus level, the best principals you know also invest in community building among the faculty, staff, students, and parents. They use mottos, vision statements, school songs, mascots, and uniforms. That's one advantage of specialized programs and schools, like having a robotics club or a school-wide focus on the performing arts. Students and teachers in those systems want to be a part of the group, and the logo on their t-shirts is an outward sign of their shared identity. Shared identity helps hold a system together.

Some people hesitate to talk about identity as a static attribute of a person or a group. We agree that we have multiple identities that develop and shift over time. We also think it is useful to focus on a shared identity within a given learning ecology at a particular moment in the life of that system.

As an example, think about what might be printed on a t-shirt, to tell the world how the group members see themselves. Here are some possibilities:

- For a language arts class: *We are readers and writers.*
- For a math class: *We are young mathematicians.*
- For a professional learning community: *We are teacher learners, supporting student inquiry.*
- For a district-wide assessment committee: *We build on students' strengths to support learning.*

Group members might also expand that identity statement into an "elevator speech." If they meet the president of the school board on the elevator, they might have 90 seconds between floors to tell her about their shared identity. What would they say?

A teacher or school leader has some authority to shape identity of a learning group. Identities, however, emerge organically over time. Additionally they can develop in unpredictable ways, based on interactions among group members. Here are questions that can help a leader think about how to influence a group's shared identity:

- Are people assigned to this group, or do they join voluntarily?
- What draws them to this group?
- Are there required expectations or mandates?
- Is this a new group, or does shared history shape a shared identity?
- What about this group and its work is exciting? engaging? inviting?
- If you are personally excited about being a part of this group, how can you share that passion with others?
- How can I set some conditions to increase the coherence of this group?

Most leaders know how to begin a learning experience with get-acquainted activities, icebreakers, and the like. But to set conditions for a learning ecology is a greater task. Those initial experiences need to do more than simply make participants comfortable. They need to invite everyone to join the team or the community. Those activities need to connect to the central work in this ecology. The activities need to build a shared identity. They build a shared sense of belonging to hold members together until they begin working as a unified whole.

An Invitation to Complex Teaching and Learning

Shared Learning Focus

What are we learning about? The need for a shared learning focus as a larger objective seems obvious. You know students who have trouble seeing the point of what they are asked to do. You have worked with teachers who either don't see a coherent focus of a professional development initiative, or they don't see it as relevant to their work. A shared learning focus addresses these challenges.

If your learning ecology is to thrive, those in the ecology need to hold a shared sense of why you are all together. They need to know what you want to learn. The leader should engage learners in conversations about what they want and need to learn. They need to invite input from the learners. Together they build a consensus related, to individual interests and to institutional and curricular goals.

In concrete terms, the learning focus might be stated as a topic, an issue, a goal, or a learner outcome. We suggest that it be stated as a question—a question to frame collaborative inquiry. A target question helps those in a learning ecology know what holds their system together. A question is a springboard for individual and collective inquiry. Various curriculum developers have used a range of terms: essential question, target question, driving question, and anchor question. In other approaches, like project-based learning, this target is framed as a problem to be solved or a solution to be designed. Each of these provides a container for the work. The learning focus, in light of who you are together, provides the container for the system.

A learning focus may be grounded in a predetermined curriculum. It should also be based on an ongoing assessment of learners' strengths and needs. It can be long-term to address the entire school year. Or the other hand you may create a short-term focus for just one topic or session. Although it is ultimately the leader's responsibility to frame the focus, learner input is important. When appropriate, setting the learning focus should be an open and collaborative process. Sometimes curricular mandates or district priorities drive the learning focus. When that's the case, the leader can adapt by using language that makes sense to the learners.

Here are questions that can help leaders develop a clear and inviting learning focus:

▶ What expectations or goals related to the learning focus are not negotiable?

▶ How does this learning focus connect to my passions? To my cultural or linguistic background? To my expertise? To my enduring questions?

▶ How do I anticipate that this learning focus will connect to my learners' passions? To their cultural or linguistic backgrounds? To their expertise? To their enduring questions?

▶ What will frame this learning experience to connect with learners' questions?

Sometimes, it is useful to "begin with the end in mind," as some curriculum developers exhort teachers to do. In other words, learners and lead learners can imagine what actions or artifacts learners might create as they move toward the learning target. Another path is to imagine a profile of the learner you want to see on completion of the learning experience. To build a shared learning focus, these target behaviors or products should be envisioned with a wide (and slightly fuzzy) lens, rather with a narrow focus on concrete products and small steps in the learning process. In other words, at this point in the process, the learning focus should be relatively general because a narrow objective may squelch diversity and discourage exploration.

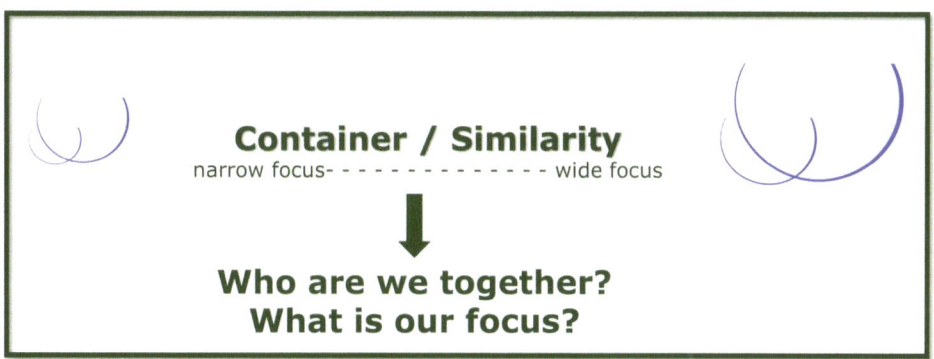

Figure 7.3. Questions form the instructional "container."

Differences that Matter

What differences are important in our learning focus? After you plan for a shared identity and focus, you can consider the task itself. Issues that matter typically indicate significant points of difference in a system. These significant differences hold the tension, or the potential energy, that may trigger movement across the system. You are never sure where or how the system will move, but it is this movement that can help new insights and new questions emerge.

Consider what you know about difference in a CAS (Module 2). First, complex systems are infinitely diverse. At the same time, at any one moment, only a few of these differences are relevant to tasks of interacting and addressing the work of the system. For example, each learner has many attributes that point to differences across the whole group—hair color, height or weight, general health, athletic prowess, reading level, interests, multilingualism, socio-economic status, family support, etc. You find, however, that not all those

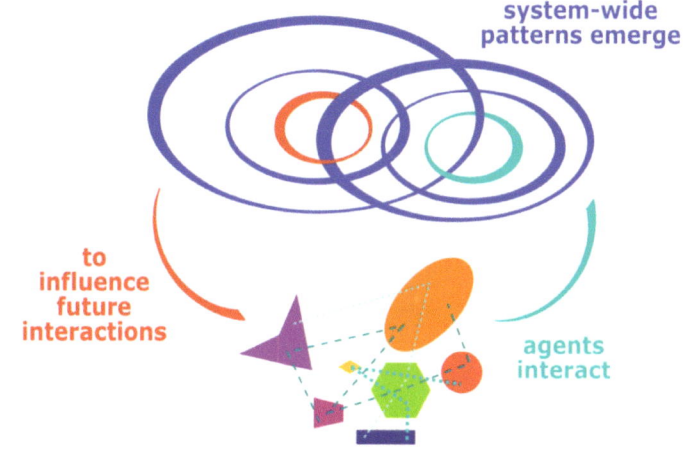

tensions are relevant to the learning focus in your ecology. As the leader, you have the power to emphasize one or more of these differences and amplify the tension it holds. But which differences will you choose?

**An Invitation to
Complex Teaching and Learning**

You know that the differences you choose have to be important enough to create tension that draws the students into the learning. At the same time the differences have to be examined in light of who might be drawn away or excluded from the learning. At the classroom level, you look for differences you see as relevant to the current focus and shared identity. You balance that with individual differences that point to inclusion and student interest. You also have the power to ignore differences that do not contribute to the learning focus.

Second, because complex systems are always evolving, patterns continually appear, disappear, change, and shift. With each shift, no matter how tiny, new differences appear (along with new similarities and connections). For example, in a third-grade learning ecology, differences between and among the children may become apparent in September. Then they may disappear or become irrelevant by November. Again, you have the power to notice, name, amplify, or ignore these emerging and shifting differences to shape the patterns you want. Changing patterns are critical in learning ecologies because they point to evidence about whether "learning" has happened. One significant difference in learning ecologies is the contrast between what learners now know and what we intend for them to know at the end of the session or semester or school year. Differences over time are relevant distinctions.

Difference provides energy for change:
➢ *choose significant differences*
➢ *note how patterns are changing*
➢ *look across levels*

Third, complex systems are nested or layered. We might notice differences within one level which may or may not be significant at other levels. In a classroom, you see daily differences within each child, depending on what happened at home the night before or what happened on the playground during recess. You also see differences, between individuals. In a grade level, you see differences among the classes, and so on. But you also notice differences between levels of the system. You see differences between one child and the whole class. You can observe differences between one class and all the classes at the grade level. You see how students at one level are different from and the rest of the campus.

In other words, these infinite differences show up in multiple ways. You can see differences individuals and groups in the system. Or you can see differences between individuals and groups in the systems. In part, what you notice depends on your focus. Is shifts with your perspective as an observer of the system. As you zoom in, you can see differences within. as you zoom out, you can see differences between people and events. Figure 7.4 reflect sources of difference that generate tension in your organization.

When you are surrounded by infinite, continually shifting differences, how do you make choices about which distinctions are relevant? When you plan to set conditions for a learning ecology to develop and grow, you need to focus on a few differences that matter.

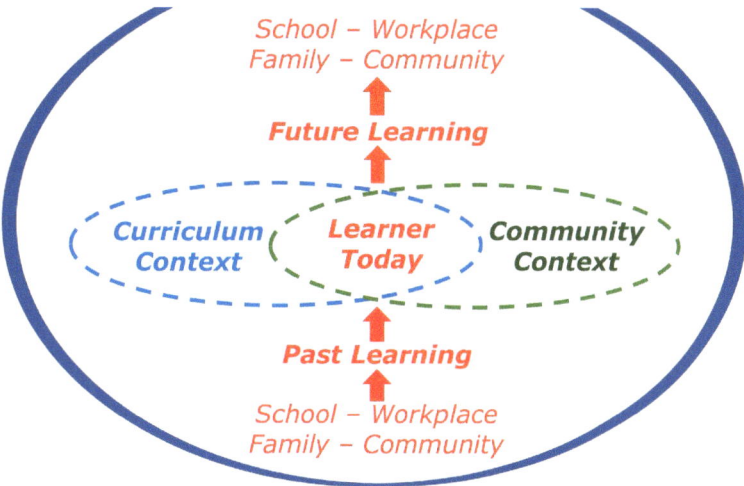

Figure 7.4. Sources of difference that generate tension in your learning ecology

You need to decide which differences might hold the energy to move the learners toward relevant insights and useful questions. In other words, which differences make a difference to learners in this ecology?

Typically, some of these decisions are handed to you in the form of policy or mandate. Some examples include: content standards, test objectives, curricular materials, performance evaluation, or assessment and accountability schemes. In other words, sometimes policy makers and administrators outside your classroom make some of the decisions about which differences make a difference. Additionally, you pay attention to parents' expectations and to community norms and traditions. These social and cultural expectations point to differences that may be relevant in the learning ecology you want to establish. Figure 7.5 represents sources of difference in a learning ecology.

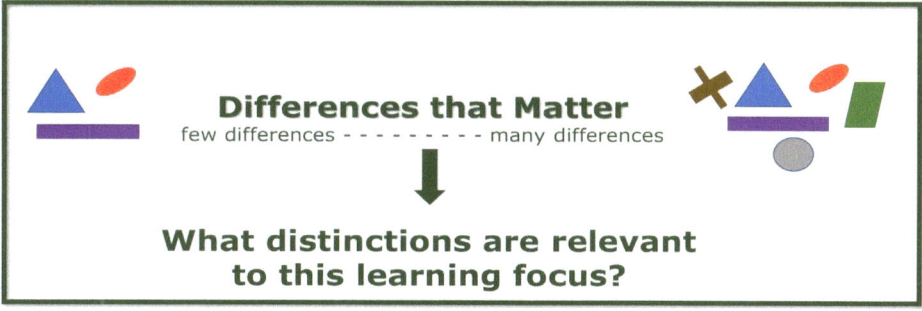

Figure 7.5. Distinctions contribute to decisions about what is important.

It's important to acknowledge these expectations. The question to ask, as you plan for specific learning ecologies, is this: What additional differences might be most generative for these individual learners and for your learning ecology over time?

An Invitation to Complex Teaching and Learning

Table 7.2. Questions about sources of difference in a learning ecology

Sources of Difference	Questions to Help Leaders Focus
Learners Today	Who are our learners—their current knowledge, skills, questions, goals, and stances?
Future Learning	What knowledge, skills, and stances do we hope the learners will acquire?
Past Learning	What are potential influences of learners' past experiences, both theory and practice?
Community Context	What are potential influences of the larger community—relevant expectations, norms, traditions and resources in the learner's community?
Curricular Context	What are potential influences of the emergent course context—relevant format, content, resources, and approach in the course?

These questions are meant as a framework for analyzing the potential differences in a learning ecology. The leader can make plans about how to focus on a few differences that will make the most difference to the identified learning focus.

Shared practices invite learners into Adaptive Action and Pattern Logic to explore differences that matter inside the learning focus.

After you brainstorm potential differences in your learning ecology, consider which distinctions are most relevant to a shared learning focus. Which distinctions:

▶ Invite learners into inquiry?

▶ Energize learning?

▶ Building supportive relationships?

▶ Best fits your hopes for your learning ecology?

What can you do to amplify and highlight those distinctions? They become the focus of instructional practices. They become the focus of Adaptive Action and Pattern Logic, as described below.

Shared Practices

How shall we use Adaptive Action and Pattern Logic? Shared practices in learning ecologies include the range of social structures that invite leaders and learners into Adaptive Action and Pattern Logic. Those two processes are foundational in learning ecologies (as explained in Module 4) because they make it possible to see, understand, and influence patterns in complex systems. Leaders engage in these practices and invite learners to watch, to participate, and, eventually, to build skill in their independent and collective inquiries. We characterize this approach to instructional leadership as inquiry-based apprenticeship, which is consistent with socio-cultural perspectives on teaching and learning (for example, Tharp & Gallimore, 1988; Lave & Wenger, 1991; Vygotsky,1978; Wilhelm, 2016).

We agree with Wilhelm, who defines inquiry as the "rigorous apprenticeship into disciplinary expertise and meaning-making" (2016, p. 58). What does that apprenticeship entail? HSD practitioners believe apprenticeship in a deep learning ecology calls the use of Adaptive Action and Pattern Logic on the differences that matter to the shared learning focus.

Figure 7.6. Shared practices ensure coherent Adaptive Actions.

Adaptive Action and Pattern Logic are the heart of teaching and learning across every discipline.

- ▶ Mathematicians notice patterns in numbers, and they create new patterns as they manipulate those numbers to solve problems.

- ▶ Artists—whether musicians, painters, dancers, sculptors, or poets—compose and perform patterns of sound, color, texture, words, and movement.

- ▶ Scientists notice and name patterns in the natural world. They hypothesize about patterns that will emerge and take action to test those hypotheses.

- ▶ Geographers focus on the interdependent patterns of topography, cartography, and culture.

- ▶ Historians' patterns are represented in timelines, charts, graphs, artifacts, and stories.

- ▶ Readers and writers make sense of patterns in language and create patterns they hope make sense to others.

- ▶ Athletes build their proficiency repeating particular patterns—actions that build strength, stamina, and strategy.

We argue that Adaptive Action and Pattern Logic are at the heart of interactions in complex human systems across disciplines both inside and outside of schools. We notice and name patterns around us—interdependent similarities, differences, and connections that carry meaning. We analyze and interpret those patterns to make sense of our experiences and to generate options for action.

- ▶ **What** do we come to know? What patterns do we notice in our observations? In our feelings? In our experiences?

- ▶ **So what** do these patterns mean? What can we infer about the underlying conditions—the similarities, the differences, and the connections?

An Invitation to Complex Teaching and Learning

▶ **Now what** shall we do to tweak those conditions in an attempt to influence the speed, direction, or nature of the emerging patterns?

Table 7.3 introduces how Adaptive Action questions are addressed in various instructional tactics.

Table 7.3. Shared practices that support your Adaptive Action.

	See Patterns *Notice and name similarities, differences, and connections related to the learning focus.*	**Understand Patterns** *Explore relationships among similarities, differences, and connections.*	**Influence Patterns** *Amplify and/or de-emphasize similarities, differences, and connections.*
Collaborative Learning Tasks	X	X	X
Read Alouds	X	X	
Science Experiments	X	X	X
Close Reading	X	X	
Writing Essays	X	X	X
Book Groups	X	X	X
What others?			

Our central question as we select and develop Shared Practices in a particular learning ecology is this: How shall we work together to use inquiry (Pattern Logic and Adaptive Action) to address our driving questions? Shared Practices will vary, depending on the age of the learners, as well as on established disciplinary practices.

Now what Four Big Questions inform your learning ecology?

Now what conditions will you set for your own learning ecology?

As you begin to consider your own deep learning ecology, consider the conditions you will set. Use these questions to guide your Adaptive Action as you make decisions how to shape the patterns you want. Use the form on the next page to consider:

▶ What is the shared identity you want to establish?

▶ What is the focus of your learning?

▶ What distinctions are relevant to that focus?

▶ What shared practices will inform your Adaptive Actions as you set conditions?

Review and reflect on the following table, and use the space allotted to document your insights and post your next questions. Use the space on this page to record your insights and reflections about what you see.

Four Big Questions	A Closer Look	Your Answers
Shared Identity *Who are we as a learning team/class?*	Who are we currently as a learning team/class? Who do we need to be? What is our desired identity? So what does this mean about moving toward a shared identity? Now what can I do to invite learners to take on a clear and coherent identity in this learning ecology?	
Shared Learning Focus *What are we learning about?*	What are we currently learning? What do we want to learn together? And what are the curricular expectations? So what will it look like when we accomplish those goals? Now what can I do to invite learners to adopt our shared learning focus?	
Relevant Distinctions *Which distinctions are relevant to our learning focus?*	Which distinctions are relevant to our learning focus? (See sources of difference above.) So what does this mean for our priorities? Now what actions can I take to focus on the differences that make a difference?	
Shared Practices *What shared practices emphasize Pattern Logic and Adaptive Action?*	What shared practices would support learners as they work toward the shared focus of learning and would also invite Pattern Logic and Adaptive Action? So what are the benefits and challenges associated with each of these practices? Now what practices should be core routines in our learning ecology and what practices can be accessible when they fit our purposes.	

Module 8
Act: Organize for Deep Learning

Inquiry is the most powerful way forward and must be part of our daily craft as reflective practitioners and professional knowledge-makers, as well as part of our work as collaborative fellow learners with students being apprenticed into the expert practices of readers, composers, and problem solvers of all kinds.

Jeffrey Wilhelm, 2016

Theoretical explanations of deep learning ecologies may be new to educators, but practical applications are not. Approaches variously labeled as "progressive," "student-centered," "inquiry-based," and "socio-cultural" are similar to Adaptive Action and Pattern Logic. They all involve iterative cycles of inquiry and reflection. Table 8.1 shares examples of familiar instructional approaches that demonstrate how teachers can set conditions for resilient and sustainable learning ecologies. And they do it without explicitly citing the principles of complex human systems:

Table 8.1. Instructional approaches that are consistent with HSD.

Instructional Approaches Consistent with HSD	
Montessori Method	http://amshq.org/
Reggio Emilia Approach	http://reggioalliance.org/
Reading Recovery	https://readingrecovery.org/
Project-Based Learning	http://www.bie.org/
National Writing Project	http://nwp.org
STEM Education	http://www.stemedcoalition.org/
Digital Literacy	http://www.connectededucators.org/
Translanguaging Classrooms	https://www.caslonpublishing.com/titles/21/translanguaging-classrooms/

**An Invitation to
Complex Teaching and Learning**

Notice this list includes approaches for adults, as well as young learners. Like HSD's approach, they engage learners in inquiry/action cycles that invite and sustain deep learning. A more thorough discussion of principles common to all these approaches can help us move beyond a superficial discussion of "how-to." Then can move toward an understanding of the transformational potential of complex learning ecologies.

What are deep learning cycles?

> **What are cycles of deep learning?**

At the center of each of these approaches is inquiry, a systematic search for patterns and a deliberate meaning-making process. It focuses on naming, analyzing, and interpreting those patterns. Inquiry cycles have been represented in different ways.

In HSD, the foundation of this process are cycles of Adaptive Action and Pattern Logic. Questions like these carry learners forward through this cycle:

- **What** do we know about this issue or topic?
- **What** patterns do we see?
- **So what** are our questions?
- **Now what** shall we do to look for answers?
- **What** facts, opinions, observations, perspectives do we find to help us answer the questions?
- **What** patterns do we see in these various data sources?
- **So what** do those patterns mean?
- **Now what** shall we do to share or use what we have learned?
- **Now what** are our new questions?

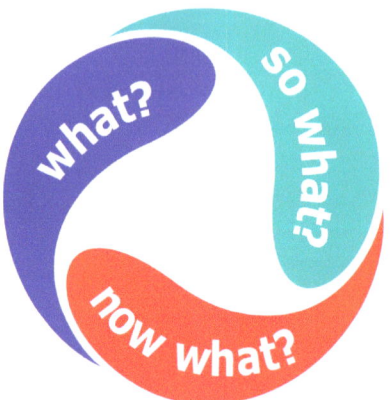

As with other representations of complex cycles, this process is recursive and reflexive. In other words, the "points on the circle" are not actually as discrete or as linear as this representation would imply. Rather than steps in a process, we think of the circles as overlapping phases in this complex learning process. In Figure 8.1, the clockwise arrows represent the general direction of the process, but learners may repeat one step or skip another, depending on their own needs and interests.

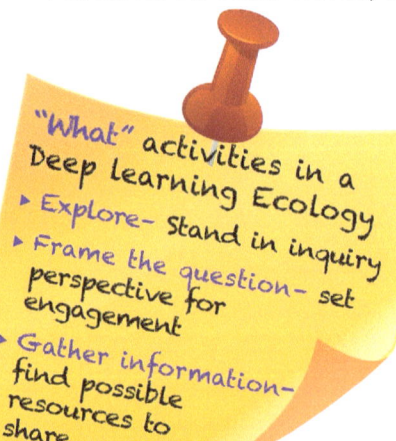

"What" activities in a Deep learning Ecology
- Explore– Stand in inquiry
- Frame the question– set perspective for engagement
- Gather information– find possible resources to share

In Figure 8.1, we explain a representation that has worked for us across multiple contexts.

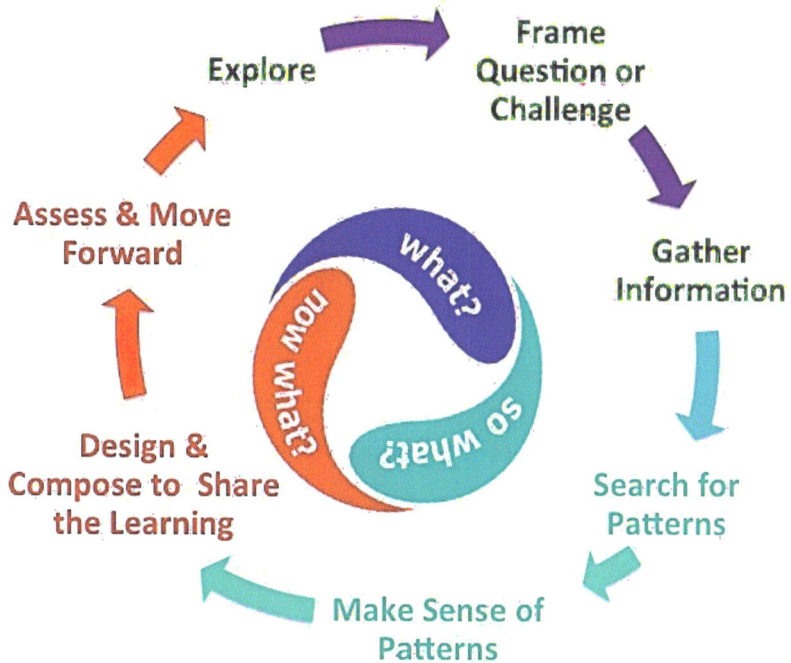

Figure 8.1. An Adaptive Action Cycle for a deep learning ecology.

In using HSD to create deep learning ecologies, the cycle in Figure 8.1 serves both leaders and learners.

▶ Leaders can use this model as a guide for instructional planning in PreK-12 classes. It can also be used for working with colleagues in a professional learning community. Leaders design instructional opportunities that take learners through the inquiry cycle in a full plan of action. Such plans, however, should be held lightly. Teaching in a learning ecology is about setting conditions and responding to learners. It's not about rigidly following a detailed set of lesson plans or instructional protocols.

▶ Learners can use this graphic as a map for navigating their inquiry journeys. It makes the process explicit. You can use it to track what learners have accomplished. Finally it sets a frame for what may come next. The following are brief explanations of each phase in the process.

What? *Explore*

Deep learning begins as you move through your life. You engage with others and explore the world. Learners with an inquiry stance will naturally explore. They see each new experience as an opportunity for learning. As a leader, you invite learners to explore their memories, current events and multiple perspectives. You invite them into a wide range of texts – printed, visual, performed, and electronic. You can ask questions, invite wonderings, and point to puzzles and anomalies. This exploration builds background knowledge and invites curiosity, which leads to the next phase of this cycle.

93

An Invitation to Complex Teaching and Learning

What? Frame the Question or Challenge

The teacher or leader usually takes the responsibility to frame the driving question of the inquiry. At the same time, wise educators know that learners' questions are always an important resource. If learners are fairly inexperienced with inquiry, the teacher can take more responsibility for framing the questions. With more experienced and confident learners, the questions can be developed collaboratively within any curricular standards. Here are general actions to help frame individual or collective inquiry:

▶ Consider the shared learning focus that, along with the shared identity of the learners, holds the ecology together (Module 7).

▶ Consider how this learning focus points to distinctions or differences that matter to this inquiry. Sometimes differences point to key issues or components of the topic and can be verbalized in many ways. (Module 7)

▶ Remember that framing the question usually includes shared experiences to activate background knowledge and invite curiosity. These experiences may build background knowledge about social, historical, political, or geographical contexts. Or experiences may be designed to review what learners have previously studied. This activates background knowledge and generates interest. You create these experiences 1) to build on cultural or linguistic knowledge, 2) to help learners see the connections between their personal experiences and the topic at hand, and 3) to frame their own question(s) for further learning.

▶ Use familiar instructional strategies to frame questions in this phase of the cycle. For example, KWL (what we **know**, what we **want to know**, and what we **learned**) is such an instructional frame (Ogle, 1986; http://www.readwritethink.org/classroom-resources/printouts/chart-a-30226.html%23related-resources). Buck Institute's Project-Based Learning process (http://www.bie.org/) also begins with a framing discussion which serves as a springboard for the project learning. Critical educators look to Freire (1970) for inspiration for a question-framing process that he calls "problem-posing." This encourages learners to "problematize" familiar texts and events to interrogate the embedded and sometimes unacknowledged power relationships embedded in our daily lives.

These are just three examples of many approaches that acknowledge the power of this question-framing phase of the inquiry teaching/learning.

The scope of the resulting questions will vary. Some will frame a long-term inquiry. Others may frame only a day or a week. Questions of more limited scope may be nested within the larger ones. Framing these nested levels of questions can help teachers make a long-term plan and see how each day or week's question can contribute to the larger inquiry.

This approach is different from totally open-ended student discovery approach (sometimes called "inquiry learning"). Rather, this inquiry-driven approach invites a deep and rigorous apprenticeship, through which the leader is a co-learner who:

- Focuses on significant questions
- Invites students to participate in the inquiry
- Offers demonstrations and explanations of the inquiry routines and skills relevant within that discipline.

Leaders may use lecture or demonstration to help learners build foundational knowledge and skills. They may invite learners into a more creative exploration of questions. The leader may step in to offer more guidance and support or may step out to provide opportunities for independent practice. Within this approach, the teacher knows what disciplinary questions should be explored and skill sets that will be most useful to learners at particular points in the inquiry.

A thorough discussion of skill sets related to inquiry is beyond the scope of this module, but here is an example. One basic skill related to inquiry is about how to ask questions. You can't assume that learners know how to ask questions well. Here are a few suggestions about how teachers can help learners improve their questioning skills:

- Always try to answer learner's questions with more refined questions. This demonstrates that the teacher is not the source of all correct answers. It also models good questioning techniques for learners.

- Try various mnemonics or instructional strategies intended to support questioning. For example, use the "Five Ws and One H" -- a journalist's foundational tool (Who, What, Where, When, Why, and How). http://blog.journalistics.com/2010/five-ws-one-h/)

- Check out particular resources designed to teach students how to ask questions. Our current favorite is a book by Rothstein, *Make Just One Change: Teach Students to Ask Their Own Questions* (2011).

All these suggestions work for professional development leaders who work with adult learners as well as educators working with younger learners. Professional learning experts have long emphasized the power of goal-setting and choice for adult learners. Leaders of professional learning frame long-term and short-term workshops, institutes, and coaching relationships. Framing professional inquiry questions involves a balance or coherence between self-selection and collective learning.

What? *Gather Information*

When learners frame their questions and challenges, they come to know what they need to learn. The next step is to gather texts and artifacts that may yield relevant information. The leader's role is to provide an array of resources and to teach learners how to access even more from a variety of sources. The leader may need to teach various skill sets that learners need to search those resources. Learners need to know how to judge credibility of sources and authenticity of information. Leaders and learners may use a variety of hard-copy and online tools to organize the information that they find.

An Invitation to Complex Teaching and Learning

Here is a partial list of resources, including written text and multimodal messages:

- Textbooks
- Websites
- Social network sites
- Videos and other multimedia texts
- Trade books (all genre)
- Interviews with subject matter experts
- Observations of nature, human systems, etc.
- Student writing
- Teacher demonstrations and lectures
- Guest speakers
- Laboratory experiments and observations
- Museums, art galleries
- Works of visual and performing art
- Reflections on personal experience
- Student-created texts

Of course, these sources can be combined in numerous ways to fit learners' needs and questions. In addition, any design would address familiar instructional decisions, like these:

- Independent, guided, or shared reading of the texts (whether print-based, digital, or other modes)
- Attention to using reading strategies that match the purpose of reading (skimming and scanning, close reading)
- Flexible grouping (whole group, small groups, pairs, individuals)
- Note-taking and note-making formats and strategies
- Opportunities for informal, formative feedback
- Critique and evaluation of source credibility

In this phase, learner activities may be similar to those in many classrooms and professional development settings. The foundational difference is that educators and learners all stand in inquiry together—searching for answers to shared questions. They create knowledge together in response to shared questions, rather than passively receiving (and memorizing) objective knowledge from experts or from the teacher.

So What? *Search for Patterns*

This phase of the cycle focuses on looking for patterns in the information learners are finding. Educators have developed a range of tools and strategies for this purpose—graphic organizers, charts, lists, for example. Patterns that help make sense of the information that learners gather might include:

- Similarities and differences
- Generalizations
- Causes and effects
- Sequences of events, or stories
- Claims and evidence

Here, we describe two tools that HSD practitioners have found particularly useful in identifying patterns like these. These foundational, yet flexible, tools for seeing, interpreting, and influencing patterns can be adapted for diverse learners across a range of age levels, disciplines, and learning tasks.

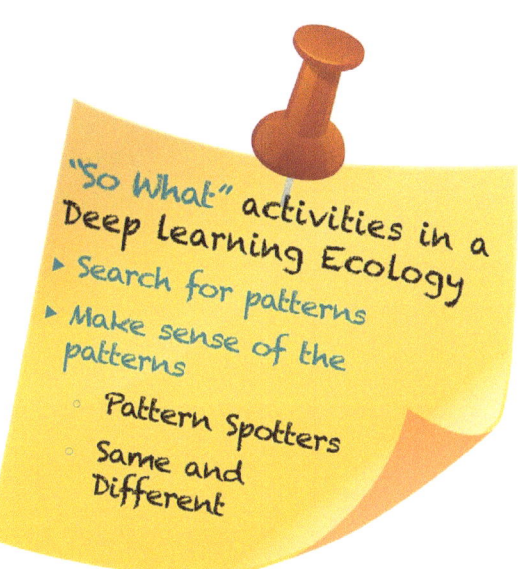

Pattern Spotters

As a tool, Pattern Spotters offers a set of questions that provide a springboard for deep thinking about the patterns in an experience, a text, or a data set. These questions can invite dialogue and generate insights by encouraging five different perspectives on a single event (Figure 8.2.).

Pattern Spotters

Generalizations *In general I notice...*

Exceptions *In general...except...*

Contradictions *On one hand...on the other hand...*

Surprises *I am surprised by...*

Puzzles *I wonder...*

Figure 8.2. Pattern Spotters—an HSD method/model to help notice and name patterns in texts, experiences and other data sets.

An Invitation to Complex Teaching and Learning

Imagine the conversations that these prompts can invite:

- ▶ **"Generalizations"** allow for a view of the whole event at once. They provide broad reactions to the whole.

- ▶ **"Exceptions"** allow you to state what you missed or what you see that didn't fit the general patterns.

- ▶ **"Contradictions"** allow you to express paradoxes you notice.

- ▶ **"Surprises"** allow you to say what happened that you didn't expect, giving voice to more potent emotions like fear and joy.

- ▶ **"Puzzles"** allow you to pose your next questions and prepare for further learning.

Dialogue generated by these questions can expand our shared understanding of a situation or set of data. In the *Making Sense* phase of the learning cycle, these questions can help individuals and groups of learners become clearer about their emerging answers to the guiding question.

Same/Different Analysis

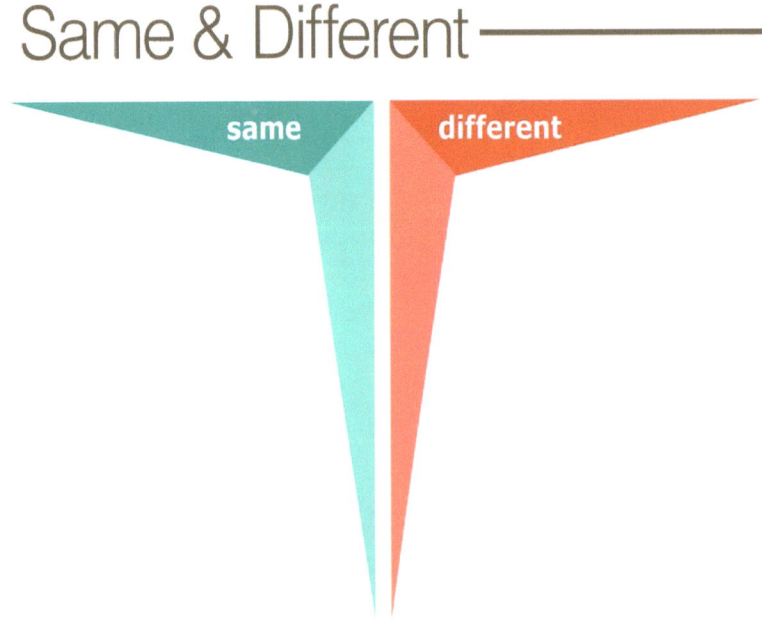

Figure 8.3. Same and Different T-chart for comparing parts of a system

A second tool, the Same/Different Analysis (Figure 8.3), is another simple way to see a basic pattern in a text, a shared experience, or in a data set. It's flexible and straightforward. It is useful even with young children. At the same time, it's also powerful enough to be useful in the analysis of district-wide test data or in policy conversations. We have even used this tool to defuse highly emotional discussions related to sensitive issues like racism and bullying.

More specifically, here are a few ways that educators might use this tool for comparing:

- ▶ Past conditions and patterns to the present observations (before and after snapshots)
- ▶ Behaviors and comments of different groups of agents
- ▶ Thoughts and feelings
- ▶ Behaviors and attitudes across scales of the system (classroom, campus, district, community)
- ▶ Primary texts written by two or more people, or at two different times
- ▶ Two or more modes or genre of texts
- ▶ Responses of two or more characters in a story
- ▶ Results in a science experiment

Now What? Design and Compose to Share the Learning

This phase of the cycle is often the culmination of the learning. It involves the creation of an artifact, text, or presentation that synthesizes findings to relevant questions or challenges. It might include both informal and formal presentations. But sometimes, learners stop in for brief opportunities to write about what they are learning. Or they meet with partners to discuss our tentative answers to the guiding questions. In addition, toward the end of the cycle (whether at the end of a day or a month), learners decide how they are going to present their findings to an audience.

- ▶ First graders may create a poster to take home to their parents
- ▶ Fifth graders may prepare a PowerPoint for a second-grade class
- ▶ Middle school poets may submit their work to a website that publishes children's poetry
- ▶ Teachers in a math institute may lead workshops for their colleagues.

This recommendation that findings be prepared with an authentic audience and real purpose in mind frames the inquiry cycle as a real-world experience. It invites authentic engagement, rather than perfunctory performance. Further, we recommend that learners explore multiple modes and genre for these presentations. More traditional academic products are sometimes appropriate and necessary. At the same time, we encourage educators to expand their notions about how learners can present and be assessed on their learning.

An Invitation to Complex Teaching and Learning

Finally, social networks, digital platforms, and community meetings provide a range of contexts where learners can share what they have learned. These venues also put the findings into action. HSD practitioners are not much interested in static knowledge as the final goal. We are more interested in how knowledge can inform action (Module 5). Figure 8.4 offers considerations about sharing what has been learned.

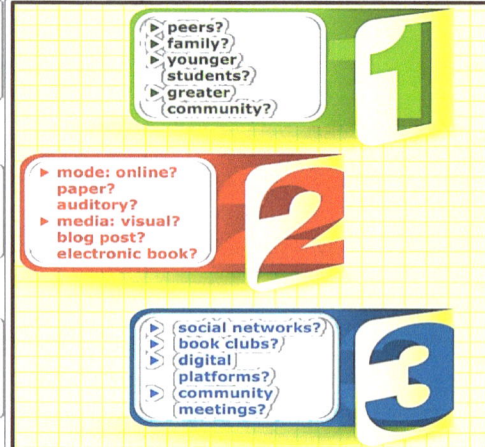

Figure 8.4. Design and compose to share the learning

A central question in a learning ecology is about how learners can take action, based on what they learn about the issue at hand. Remember that Adaptive Action is the heart of this inquiry cycle. It is always our hope that learning will lead to options for action. Our extended hope is that those actions can ultimately address real-world problems.

Now What? Assess and Move On

Finally, this is the place in the cycle where we can embed tools for assessment (both self-assessment and external assessment). These assessments will work differently across age and grade levels. Also, it will be different in a professional learning setting from the PreK-12 classroom.

Each iteration of an Adaptive Action cycle leads into the next question, the next opportunity to gather data, and the next pattern analysis. That is clearly the case whenever Adaptive Action is the foundation for a learning ecology. The Adaptive Action questions can be used as a framework for self-assessment:

- What did we learn? What did we accomplish?
- So what does this mean? Is it what we wanted or expected?
- Now what are our new questions or goals?
- Now what is our next step?

In this phase of Now What:

- ▶ A faculty study group will decide on the next book they want to read together.
- ▶ A fifth grader will set goals for improving his writing in the next grading period.
- ▶ After a study of mammals, a third-grade science class will generate a set of questions about how mammals are different from reptiles and amphibians.
- ▶ Based on their study of the U.S. Civil Rights Movement in the 1960s, high school history students generate a list of questions about civil rights in the present day.

Each cycle leads into the next, in what we hope becomes a generative life-long learning journey.

So what are deep learning cycles across the system?

This deep learning cycle, with Adaptive Action and Pattern Logic at the center, can be the engine that drives teaching and learning at all scales of the system. This is true in classrooms and professional learning initiatives. It also holds true in program implementation, community relations, and all system decisions.

> **So what do deep learning cycles look like across the system?**

As we conclude this discussion, we want to emphasize that this cycle can be the engine for system-wide improvement of policies and practices. The driving questions and challenges of system policies address ways to support student learning. When everyone inquires authentically into those questions, those inquiry cycles build adaptive capacity and sustainability for instruction throughout the system. Ultimately what is learned in those inquiry cycles holds the potential for improving student learning over the long term (Figure 8.5).

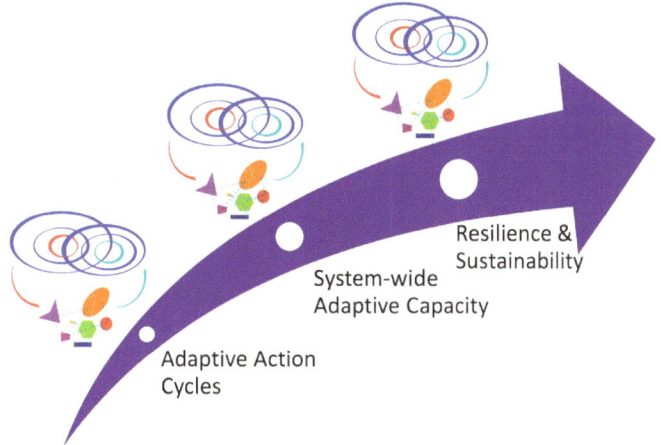

Figure 8.5. Deep Learning Cycles build system-wide adaptive capacity, resilience, and sustainability

An Invitation to
Complex Teaching and Learning

Multiple inquiry cycles are clearly at work in many of the inquiry-based approaches like those listed at the beginning of this module. One example is Reading Recovery (for example, Clay, 1991). In daily one-to-one sessions the teacher invites the child to read and write. The teacher closely observes and prompts the young reader to use meaning, structure, and visual cues to read the carefully selected texts. That same encouragement supports the child in writing brief messages.

Guiding questions focus on "What makes sense? What sounds right? What looks right?" The student engages in inquiry. The Reading Recovery Teacher inquires into what each reader knows and what learning is needed next. The Reading Recovery Teacher Leader inquiries into what works with a number of teachers. She problem-solves with them and observes what each teacher need to learn as they support their learners. The Site Coordinator focuses on implementation issues across a school district. University Reading Recovery trainers engage in inquiry, supporting multiple ongoing inquiries in each district, campus, and Reading Recovery session. The Teacher Leader and the Reading Recovery trainers continue working with children. They never lose sight of this foundational inquiry process and how to support children who are learning to read.

In a system-wide deep learning ecology, there is a common belief and commitment of everyone throughout the system: Current knowledge is always tentative. Close observation and interpretation are essential to making decisions about our next wise actions.

Of course, it's less demanding to follow the steps in a commercial instructional program. It's easier to follow the leads of your team members, using lesson plans that are "tried and true." It's simpler to take a mechanical perspective, to "implement with fidelity" an instructional scheme that was developed for other learners, in another school, in a community far away from yours. The HSD approach attempts to set conditions for organic, unpredictable, and complex learning. It not without risks and demands. Anais Nin suggests that the risk is worthwhile and, even, necessary.

> *And the day came when the risk to remain tight in a bud was more painful than the risk it took to blossom.*

Now what shapes my deep learning cycle?

Now what will my deep learning cycles look like?

Use the table on the next page to begin to map a deep learning cycle in your learning ecology. Use the questions to consider what will be happening for you and for the learners in your system.

Cycle Phase	Consider	What will the Teacher do?	What will the Learner do?
Explore	▶ Read widely ▶ Observe closely ▶ Move beyond class into community & natural environment		
Frame Question or Challenge	▶ Consider students' interests & wonderings ▶ Survey significant issues & questions ▶ Refer to curricular standards		
Gather Information	▶ Search primary sources (observation, interviews, document analysis, etc.) ▶ Search secondary sources (print, electronic, multimodal) ▶ Guide students' note taking & organizational strategies		
Search for Patterns	▶ Guide students' analysis (thematic? cause-effect? chronological? other?) ▶ Encourage students to summarize & synthesize		
Make Sense of Patterns	▶ Guide student' personal response, interpretation, evaluation ▶ Help students consider options for graphic representation		
Design & Compose to Share the Learning	▶ Consider audience and occasion (small-group discussion? multimodal presentations? written products? other?)		
Assess & Move Forward	▶ Consider teacher assessment procedures ▶ Consider self-assessment procedures		

Module 9
Decision: When to Step in and When to Step Out

> . . . no instructional approach will work for all students . . . (The teachers we observed) attempted to build on the identities, knowledge, and skills that each student brought to the classroom.
>
> Patterson, Wickstrom, Roberts, Auaujo, Hoki

The educator's role in a learning ecology is complex. First, they are instructional designers, choosing and shaping the learning context, materials, and tasks. They are also lead learners, standing beside their student apprentices in shared inquiry. But, much like parents, their long-term goal is to move learners toward independence. The personal goal is to move themselves into obsolescence. Ultimately, teachers in learning ecologies look forward to the time that their learners will no longer need them.

What is just enough support for a learner?

Given that goal, the teacher's continuing challenge is knowing when to move in and offer more support, and when to move out to allow learners to struggle a little. They support the learner to take the inevitable risks that lead to independent and productive inquiry. Educational theorists, researchers, and practitioners have grappled with this question for centuries. Rousseau, Montessori, Dewey, Vygotsky, and Bruner are just a few of the people who have contributed to this ongoing conversation. In HSD, we can say with confidence that the answer to this question is this: It depends!

> **What informs decisions about supports for diverse learners?**

As we explained in previously, Leaders interact not only with learners in learning ecologies, but also with the resources, materials, expectations, and other contextual issues. The representation below (Figure 9.1) of a complex adaptive system reminds us about how those interactions generate patterns unique to that system. Remember that those emergent patterns, in turn, influence or constrain subsequent interactions.

An Invitation to Complex Teaching and Learning

The lead learner's decisions are represented by some of the arrows and lines between the participants, texts, and other actors in the system at the bottom of the figure. That's where lead learners design instructional experiences, demonstrate target behaviors, ask probing questions, provide timely feedback, and much more.

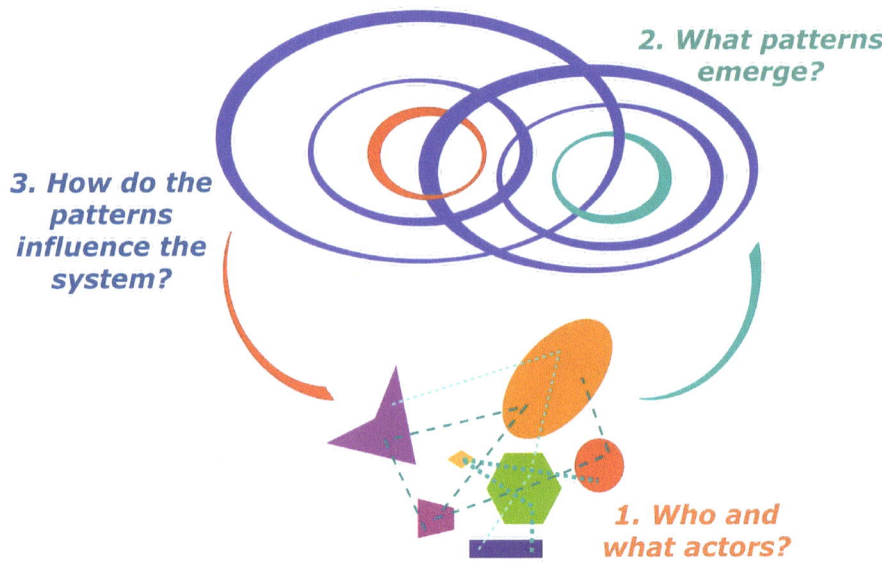

Figure 9.1. Understand your complex adaptive system (CAS)

The questions addressed in this module are about the nature of those interactions:

- ▶ How much supportive structure (sometimes called scaffolding) should I provide my learners?
- ▶ How often should I provide feedback, and what should that feedback look like?
- ▶ How much should I allow and encourage peer collaboration?
- ▶ How should I allow or encourage bilingual learners to use multiple languages?
- ▶ What kinds of materials and resources should I make available? How easy or difficult should those materials be for individual learners?

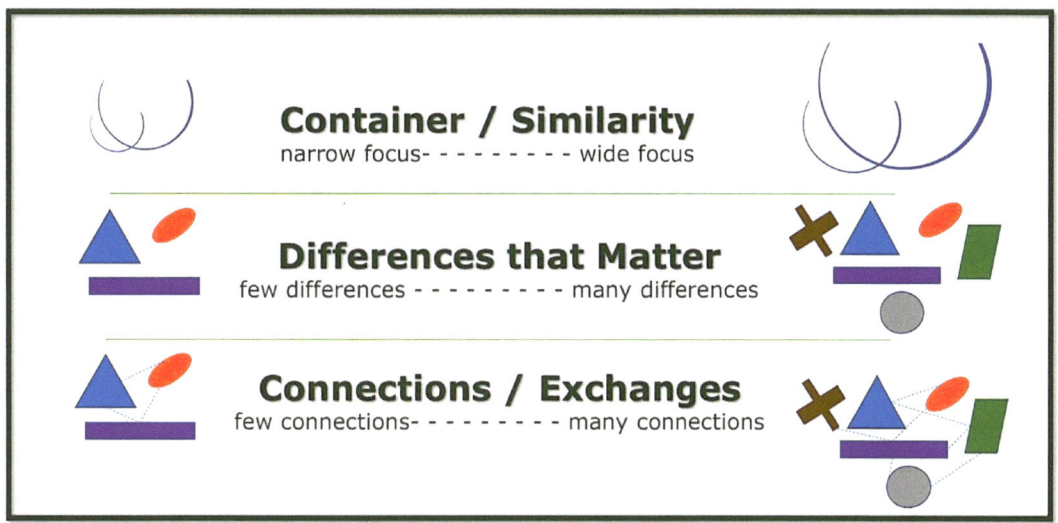

Figure 9.2. Range of options can shift conditions of self-organizing dynamics

Figure 9.2 suggests options for action—how lead learners can change the conditions and provide more or less support for learners. As each condition is changed, the interactions will be different, and the emergent patterns may shift. Of course, the important emergent patterns in a learning ecology are the learner outcomes. So instructional moves that tighten the container, reduce the potential number of differences, or focus the exchanges will provide more support (scaffolding) for learners. When learners are ready to be more independent, the instruction can be less focused, more open-ended (Figure 9.2). The ongoing question is how leaders make these decisions. How do they know when to step in to offer support and when to step back to let learners work independently?

What is the Landscape Diagram?

HSD practitioners use a model called the Learning Landscape Diagram to think more specifically about how much and what kinds of support learners might need. Think of learning possibilities as a landscape that a learner can navigate, encountering some challenges that are easy and others that are difficult. Imagine that this learning landscape can be mapped at the intersection of two dimensions:

What is the landscape of learning in my classroom?

- ▶ **Certainty** of the content refers to objectivity: How certain is the content? How likely is it that there is just one "right" answer?

- ▶ **Predictability** of the content: How predictable is the content for learners? How familiar it is to them?

The HSD Learning Landscape uses these two dimensions to map options for teaching and learning (Figure 9.3).

An Invitation to Complex Teaching and Learning

Figure 9.3. Landscape Diagram maps potential interactions and decisions in a complex system

If learning objectives are narrowly focused on just a few ideas (one right answer), the content is more certain, and it is easier for the learners to grasp. If the content is very familiar to them and more predictable, it is also easier for the learners. That certain and predictable part of the learning landscape is represented in the bottom left of the diagram. Examples would be math facts, spelling lists, and other memorization or rote work. The more uncertain (more possibilities for right answers) and the less predictable (less familiar to the learner) the content is, the more challenging it is for particular learners. That extreme is represented in the top right of the diagram. Examples of those types of learning might include open-ended problem solving, creativity, and personal interpretation or analysis.

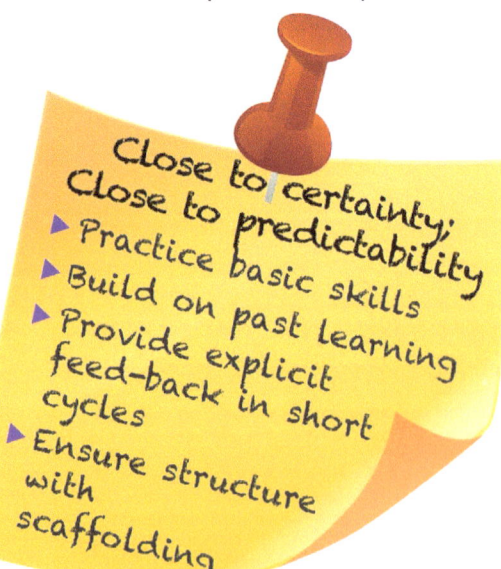

The following descriptions reflect how the diagram would point to different approaches, depending on the experience of the learners.

Professional Development Leaders:

▶ Beginning teachers need information about procedures and teaching techniques. For them, a PD leader might plan workshops with a great deal of structure. There would also be a narrow focus on classroom management systems or grading procedures. (close to predictable and close to certainty)

▶ For experienced teachers, a PD leader might use book studies or inquiry groups. Those learning opportunities offer less structure and more open-ended invitations. (far from predictable and far from certainty)

Teachers:

▶ When working with 11th and 12th graders in a college prep program, teachers typically plan instruction that fits in the in the upper right. The recognize they need to encourage students to develop independence. (far from predictable and far from certainty)

▶ Teachers working with recent immigrants need to focus on vocabulary and language for social interactions. They may want to begin at the lower left of the diagram, beginning with simple tasks and building on the English students already know. (close to predictable and close to certainty)

This Learning Landscape is a thinking tool—not an answer machine!
Remember this tool doesn't offer a formula. Leaders' specific decisions are always dependent on the task, the context, and the learners themselves. A single learner can need different kinds of support at different times. Typically, when any learner—even a highly skilled learner—encounters something new and challenging, she needs supportive instructional activities in the bottom left of the Learning Diagram. On the other hand, any learner—even a struggling student—can be productive in the upper right of the Learning Diagram when she has relevant experience.

If content objectives are too easy, learners get bored. If they are too divergent or unpredictable, learners give up. Educators working with PreK-12 students or adults search for instructional options that offer the "just right" balance between those two extremes. In a deep learning ecology, the balance between these two extremes points to what Vygotsky called the zone of proximal development (ZPD):

. . . the distance between the actual developmental level as determined by independent problem solving and the level of potential development as determined through problem solving under adult guidance, or in collaboration with more capable peers (Vygotsky, 1978, p. 86).

The ZPD, or the learning zone, refers to the central area of this landscape diagram. The learning is challenging enough that the learner cannot function independently, yet the learner can be successful with assistance. It's not too easy and not too difficult. In the ZPD, the learner is stretching to the next most difficult outcome, with assistance and support.

So what does this mean for a lead learner's decisions?

So how do you decide when to use a more constrained, concrete approach and when to use an approach that is less constrained, more open ended? The figure below helps you visualize this "landscape" of possible instructional decisions.

So what does this mean about decisions I make?

An Invitation to Complex Teaching and Learning

A more constrained approach (bottom left) would include direct instruction, drill and practice, memorization, computation. These approaches move toward one correct answer. On the other hand, a less constrained approach (top right) would include creativity, trial and error, and open-ended inquiry. Although each of those extremes may fit particular tasks or challenges, most instruction falls somewhere between.

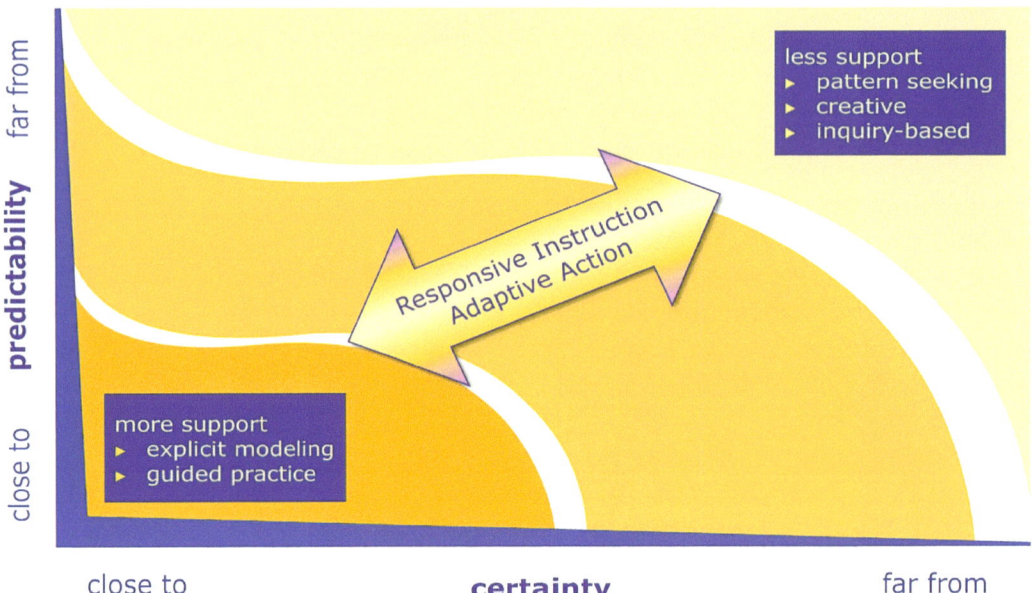

Figure 9.4. Learning Landscape Diagram represents range of instructional options

Always, instructional decisions should be based on an understanding of human learning as a complex system. It is open, diverse, and nonlinear. Lead learners who are watching the patterns emerge over time can work with those complex dynamics. They don't have to try to predict or control them. Notice how these questions integrate Adaptive Action and Pattern Logic:

- **What** patterns do I see within and between learners?
- **What** are their strengths and targets, in reference to the desired learning outcomes?
- **What** can they do independently?
- **What** can they accomplish with support?
- **So what** do these patterns mean? Do these learners need more or less convergent content or more or fewer predictable experiences to support their increasing independence?
- **Now what?** What instructional actions can I take to best support these learners?
  - Smaller containers?
  - Fewer differences?
  - Tighter connections or interactions?

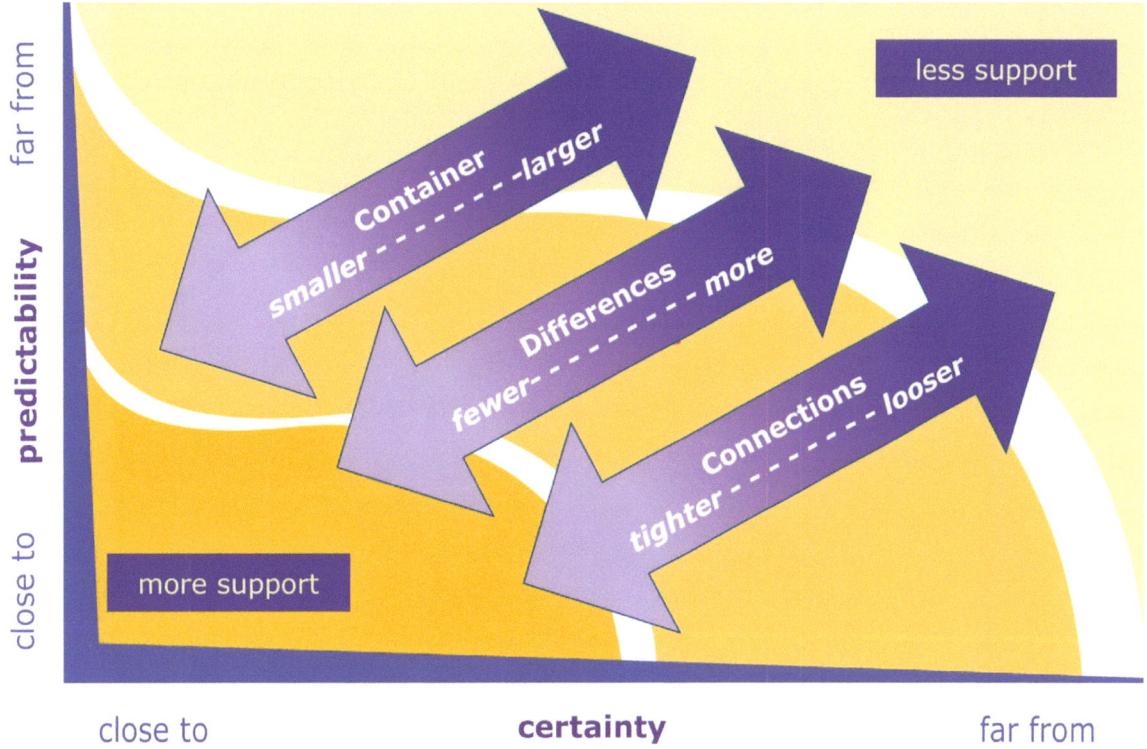

Figure 9.5. Learning Landscape Diagram suggests options to shift conditions for deep learning

Educators may recognize this explanation as a general rationale for what is typically called "gradual release of responsibility" (Pearson & Gallagher, 1983):

- ▶ I do (teacher demonstration)
- ▶ We do (shared and guided practice)
- ▶ You do (independent practice)

Sometimes, however, that approach is interpreted in a much-too linear way, assuming that teachers should always begin instruction in the lower left of the landscape diagram and move toward the upper right as students gain more experience and expertise. But it is not always that simple. You might want to begin in the upper right, both to explore a topic and to build some curiosity. When the learners generate questions, then you can move toward the lower left for some craft lessons, some skill-building, or some group work that helps them answer their questions.

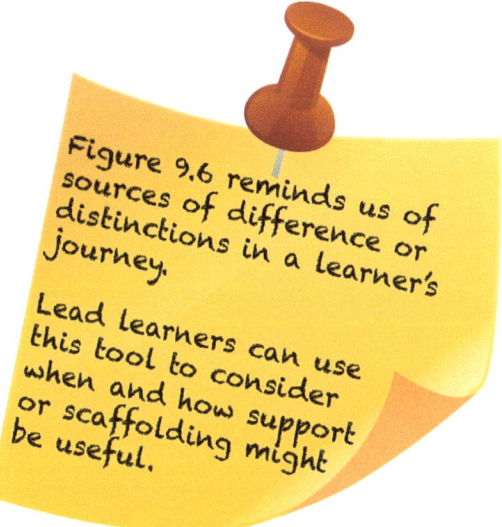

Figure 9.6 reminds us of sources of difference or distinctions in a learner's journey.

Lead learners can use this tool to consider when and how support or scaffolding might be useful.

An Invitation to Complex Teaching and Learning

The Learning Landscape—in all its iterations—resists instructional dichotomies, for example, the tendency to label instructional methods as either "teacher-directed" or "student centered." The most powerful teaching and learning is more complex than that. It happens as the lead learner fluently moves around the Learning Landscape, using various instructional models, as appropriate, to offer structure and support in response to learners' next steps.

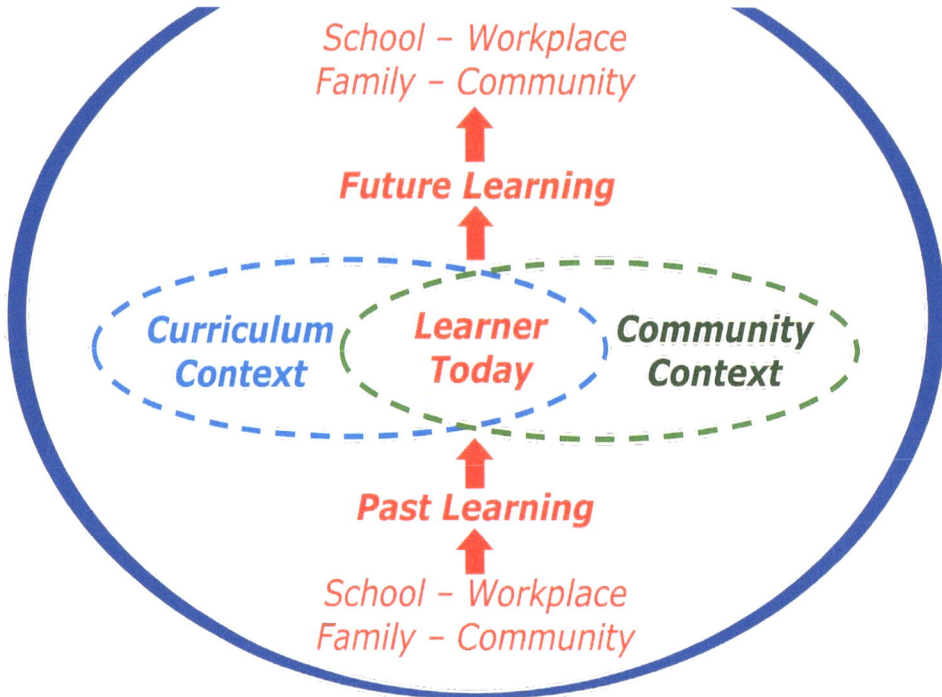

Figure 9.6. Sources of difference

The learner support in instructional models may come from sources other than the teacher. For example, from the task itself, from the texts that are chosen, or from peer collaboration. You design the lesson and provides resources, but you may not personally offer the direct support. When you consider when and how these constraints can support student progress in a learning ecology, you can see how instructional decisions will either increase or decrease constraints.

The learning magic is not in so-called "fidelity of implementation of best practices." It is actually in the skill and insight in a teacher's judgment. Effective teachers know about how to shift conditions in the learning ecology to shift constraints as needed. The table below translates the Learning Landscape into suggestions about decisions teachers make. They judge where to step in and offer support and where to step back and let learners build independence. Not all questions are relevant to every instructional decision, but each one suggests ways teachers can respond, based on differences across the class.

Table 9.1. Table of instructional decisions, based on Learner Landscape

	Leaders Set Constraints that Fit the Purpose	**More or less similarity?**	**Fewer or more differences?**	**Tighter or looser connections?**
Learners Today	Who are our learners—their current knowledge, skills, questions, goals, and stances?	Whole group? Small group? Pairs? Individual?	Emphasize shared attributes? Emphasize learner differences?	Nurture relationships? Increase independence?
Future Learning Goals	What knowledge, skills, and stances do we hope the learners will acquire?	Emphasize a single learning focus? Emphasize multiple learning goals?	Emphasize a range of diverse kinds of knowledge, experience, and expertise?	Design tight or loose feed-back loops?
Past Learning	What are potential influences of learners' past experiences, both theory and practice?	Decide on the appropriate range of past learning experiences	Include global connections	Invite learners to reflect on past experiences as springboards for future learning?
Community Context	What are potential influences of the larger community--relevant expectations, norms, traditions, and resources in the learner's community?	Focus on school culture? Include family and community?	Emphasize specific kinds knowledge, experiences, expertise?	Make opportunities for learners to interact with people in the community?
Curricular Context	What are potential influences of the emergent course context—relevant format, content, resources, and approach in the course?	Tight content focus? Wider content focus, even interdisciplinary connections?	Explicit connections across concepts? Few connections across concepts?	One-size-fits-all instruction? Differentiated instruction?

An Invitation to Complex Teaching and Learning

Now what will the landscape be for your learning ecology?

Use the Learning Landscape Diagram and this protocol to analyze a teaching challenge you currently face.

> **Now what will my learning landscape offer?**

1. **What?** Take five minutes and describe a teaching challenge you are facing—as a teacher in a K-12 classroom or as an administrator or instructional coach in a professional learning setting. Reflect on the learner, the patterns you are seeing, the learning goal(s), a recent task or situation, and the challenge.

2. **So What?** Use the Learning Landscape Diagram to make sense of the patterns you are seeing in relation to whether the conditions are exerting an appropriate level of constraints to trigger self-organization and learning.

   ▶ Does the recent challenge result suggest that the learning is over constrained? If so, how might you invite the learner into a situation that is less constrained?

   OR

   ▶ Does the recent challenge result suggest that the learning is under constrained? If so, how might you invite the learner into a situation that is more supportive, where the constraints are tighter?

3. **Now what?** Brainstorm for three actions you might take to shift the conditions and change the constraints within this learning ecology?

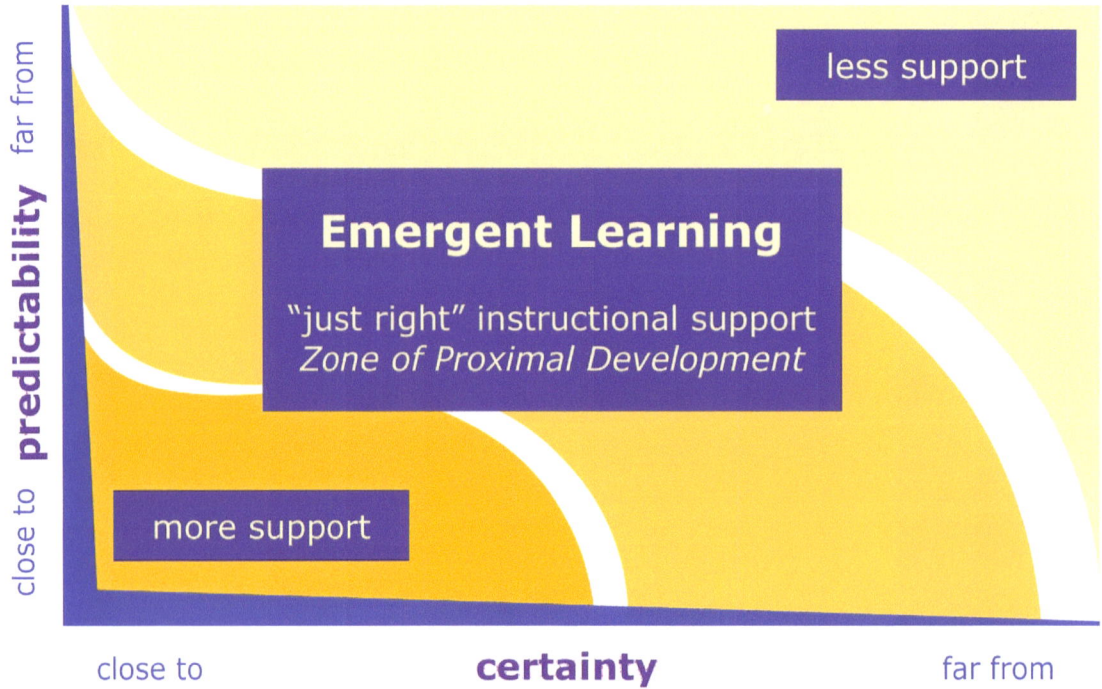

Module 10
The Task: Build Coherence

[Science] is more than a school subject, or the periodic table, or the properties of waves. It is an approach to the world, a critical way to understand and explore and engage with the world, and then have the capacity to change that world..."
— President Barack Obama

What is manifold is often frightening because it is not neat and simple. Men prefer to forget how many possibilities are open to them."
— Martin Buber

In a healthy school system, everyone is a learner. Everyone engages in praxis. They integrate theory and practice as they adapt to whatever challenges arise. Praxis, when it includes Adaptive Action and Pattern Logic, holds the potential for ongoing adaptation and learning. That says there is hope for K-12 school systems to improve teaching and learning continually throughout the system—at least as long as educators attend to system dynamics in their learning ecology.

In HSD, we would say that a school district where educators across the system use Adaptive Action to influence patterns has *adaptive capacity*. We define adaptive capacity as the ability to use inquiry, reflection, and action to respond appropriately and to adapt to whatever comes their way.

The question is, first, how to invite educators and students into such a learning ecology. The second question is how to sustain that adaptive work, even in the face of challenges like changing personnel, new policy mandates, and shrinking budgets. This module addresses the sustainability of this work. Sustainability is connected to the four patterns introduced earlier as signs of a healthy, self-sustaining learning system: diversity, coherence, adaptive capacity, and interdependence (Figure 10.1).

These interdependent patterns are what anyone would want to see in their learning ecologies, whether at the classroom, campus, or district levels. One way HSD practitioners set conditions for these adaptive and self-sustaining patterns is by applying a set of Simple Rules throughout the system. Review Figure 10.1 and consider the different patterns as you read about Simple Rules.

An Invitation to Complex Teaching and Learning

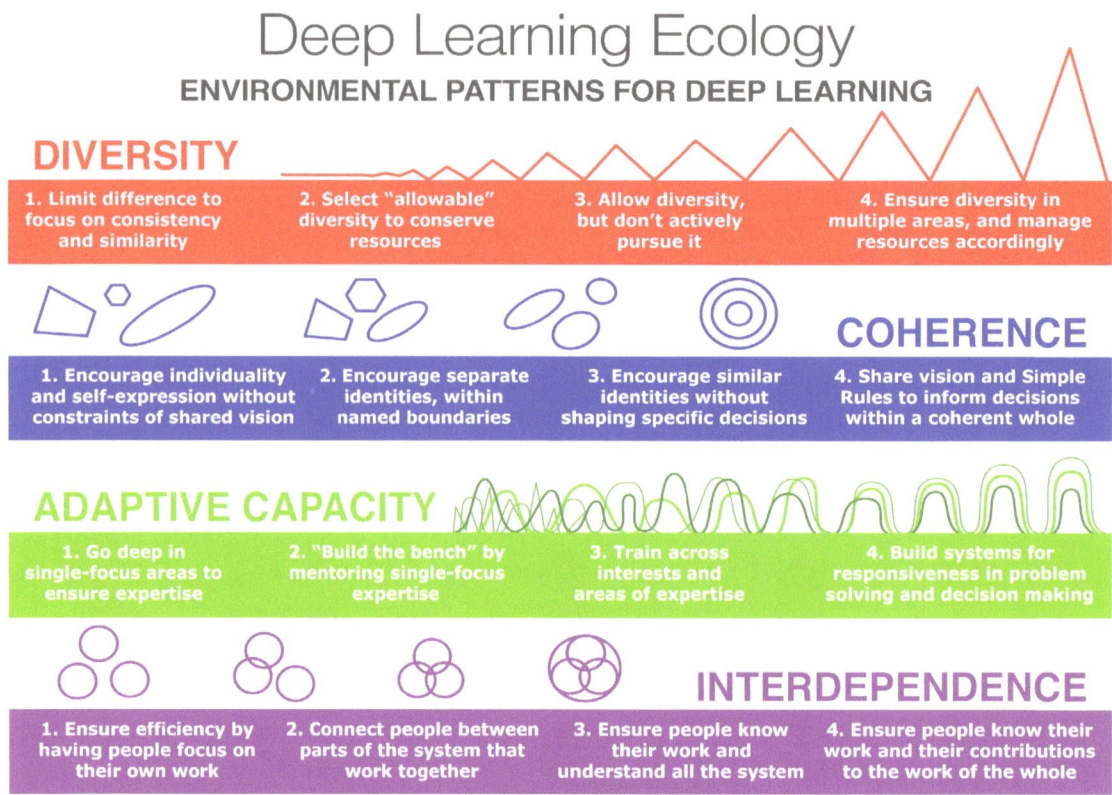

Figure 10.1. Creating the essential patterns of a deep learning ecology.

What are Simple Rules?

What guides our decisions around here?

In complex adaptive systems (in nature and in human societies), scientists have noticed that when individual agents work together according to a set of shared rules or expectations, larger patterns emerge across the whole system (for example, Holland, 1998). These expectations may be tacit, or they may be explicit.

In human systems, we have learned that we can use simple rules to establish coherent patterns across the whole. Simple Rules are clear and straightforward behavioral expectations that everyone in the system agrees to follow. Figure 10.2 reflects how Simple Rules shape dominant patterns across a system.

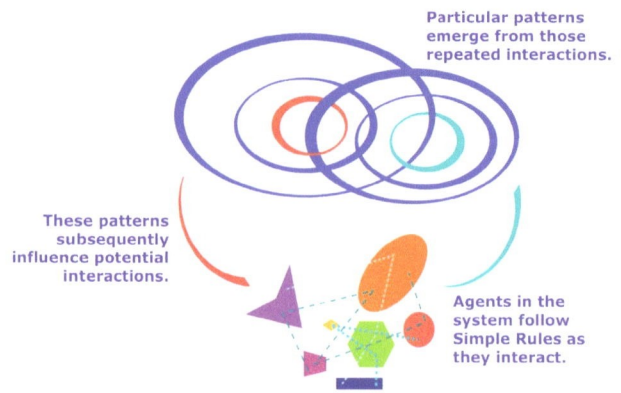

Figure 10.2. Simple Rules influence emergent patterns in human systems.

In the 1980s, mathematicians began to explore what causes large groups to move in shared patterns. They studied birds flocking, fish swimming in schools, and humans moving quickly across shared space. They proposed the idea of simple rules, stating that members in these groups follow a shared set of "rules" that guide their decision making, relative to the large group. In 1986, Craig Reynolds first demonstrated the way simple rules work, creating a computer simulation of flocking birds. (For an explanation, see https://www.youtube.com/watch?v=QbUPfMXXQIY.) In this case of flocking, the simple rules he posed are about alignment, coherence, and avoidance:

- Fly the same direction as the rest of the flock
- Match the speed of the other members of the flock
- Don't run into anyone

Of course, human behavior is much more complex birds flocking, but in human systems you see simple rules at work in cultural or social norms. Brian Sauser's video (https://youtu.be/-fl4xOWMbYs) illustrates how simple rules work in human systems. Any group of people who live, work or play together have spoken and unspoken agreements about how they relate to one other and how they do their work. For example,

- Keep to the right (in the US) if you move more slowly than those around you.
- Do unto others as you would have them do unto you.
- Don't rock the boat.
- Work hard and take care of business.
- Tell the truth only when it benefits you.

As this list of examples suggests, some simple rules can be useful and support generative learning. On the other hand, some simple rules can generate dysfunctional patterns. In HSD, we have identified a set of simple rules that have proven useful to create patterns of generative learning. We don't believe this is the only set of rules that might be useful. We do believe when people attend to these simple rules to guide their decision making and interaction, they set conditions for generative patterns. We call these the "Radical Rules" because they can influence the deepest interactions of teaching and learning (Patterson, Holladay, & Eoyang, 2013).

- Teach and learn in every interaction.
- Attend to whole, the part, and the greater whole.
- See, understand, and influence patterns.
- Recognize and build on assets
- Seek the true and the useful.
- Act with courage.
- Engage in joyful practice.

An Invitation to Complex Teaching and Learning

Clearly, these rules can apply in every situation across the system: in personal relationships; in the classroom, in campus teams, in a superintendent's cabinet, among school board members, in parent conferences, and so on. We have also noticed that this particular set of Simple Rules tends to generate patterns that support and sustain learning. In their classroom research, colleagues in the North Star of Texas Writing Project documented particular learning patterns in language arts classrooms (Patterson, Wickstrom, Roberts, Araujo, and Hoki, 2010):

Table 10.1. Aspirational patterns emerge when learners engage in particular actions

Aspirational Patterns in Learning Ecologies	
These patterns emerge...	*When learners...*
Empathy	Take multiple perspectives, imagining how others think and feel.
Inquiry	Build capacity to make sense of the world—the past, present, and future.
Dialogue	Embrace uncertainty—noticing and interpreting patterns.
Authenticity	Eagerly engage in tasks learners see as significant.
Apprenticeship	Work with peers and teachers as they build confidence and expertise.
Re-visioning	Reflect, assess, and take informed action to adapt to changing conditions.

These patterns emerge as teachers and students behave in the ways described in the table. They may not have had conversations about this as a set of Simple Rules, but it's clear their shared understandings and shared practices are coherent with the spirit of these rules.

Conversations about these simple rules and generative patterns have helped participants get to know one another, build shared definitions, tell stories about their experiences, and move forward to strengthen their individual and collective work. The specific language is always negotiable, and some groups have found more appropriate ways to word these ideas for their situation. The number of rules can vary as well. Some decide to use only four of the rules or only three of the patterns.

We have found that it is important for Simple Rules to offer answers to the Four Big Questions in Module 7:

- ▶ Who we are together?
- ▶ What is our shared focus?
- ▶ What matters in this system?
- ▶ How shall we work together?

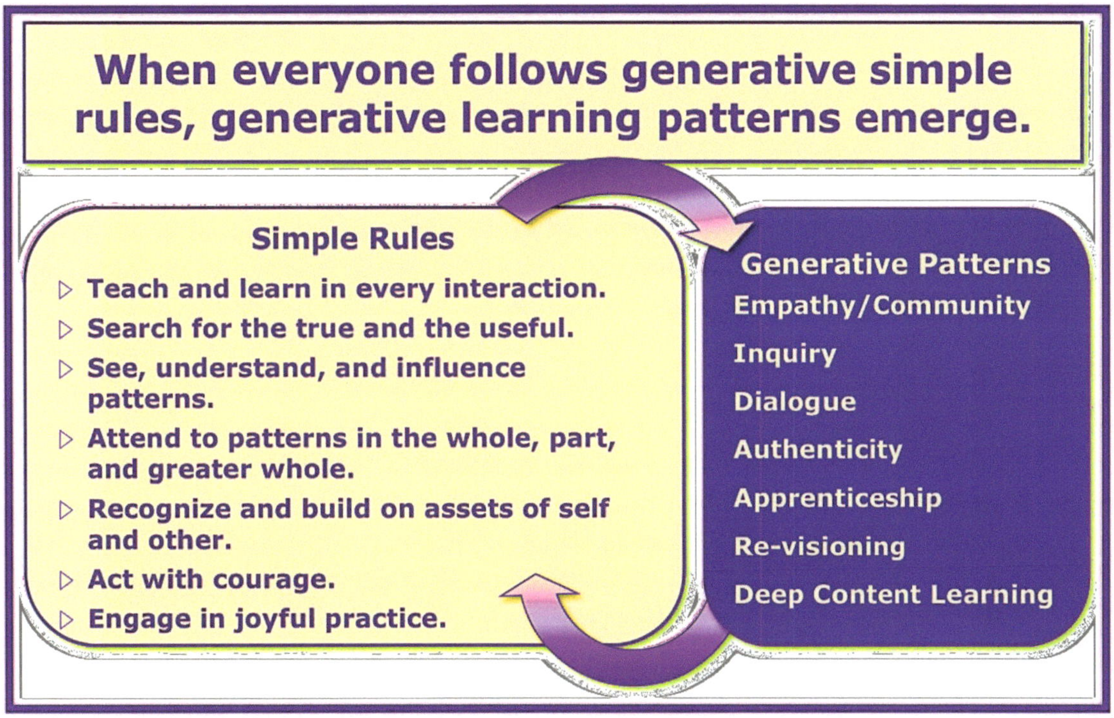

When everyone follows generative simple rules, generative learning patterns emerge.

Simple Rules
- Teach and learn in every interaction.
- Search for the true and the useful.
- See, understand, and influence patterns.
- Attend to patterns in the whole, part, and greater whole.
- Recognize and build on assets of self and other.
- Act with courage.
- Engage in joyful practice.

Generative Patterns
Empathy/Community
Inquiry
Dialogue
Authenticity
Apprenticeship
Re-visioning
Deep Content Learning

Figure 10.3. When people in a system follow a shared set of rules, shared patterns can emerge from their interactions

Sometimes those four questions can help groups think about a possible set of simple rules. The bottom line is that Simple Rules adopted by a group should build shared agreements about what they are doing together and what they value as partners in this learning ecology.

So how do Simple Rules help build adaptive capacity for systemic change?

Adaptive capacity is the capability of a learning system to sense, interpret, and use information continually in response to changing conditions within or outside the system. It is the ability to build resilience and sustainability. In other words, adaptive capacity increases as people learn to use Pattern Logic and Adaptive Action to influence conditions to shape particular patterns in the system. Adaptive capacity in the larger system increases as more individuals learn to set conditions for generative learning in more places in the system.

> **So what do Simple Rules do to help build Adaptive Capacity for systemic change?**

It is probably clear by now that, in HSD, we define learning as adaptation. Adaptive Action (**What? So What? Now What?**) is the essential structure of deep learning. When everyone in the system—individually and collectively—engages in Adaptive Action over the long haul, individual and systemic learning will inevitably happen. When Adaptive Action is happening throughout the system, the system develops adaptive capacity, which, in turn, leads to resilience and sustainability.

An Invitation to
Complex Teaching and Learning

The central irony about adaptive capacity is this: The emergent patterns are not always productive or generative. The patterns that emerge are shaped by the conditions that are set. Painful and uncomfortable patterns can be reinforced and sustained if conditions are set to generate those kinds of patterns. For instance, if the system or the leader sets conditions that reward competition isolation, those patterns form. As participants in the system, each learner and lead learner has the power to influence those conditions and generate local patterns that may or may not match the patterns in the larger system. That's why, even in the more progressive school, you can have one teacher whose classroom is different from the rest. The trick is to 1) pay attention to the patterns you see, 2) decide whether they are similar to what you want to see, and 3) take small actions to adjust the local conditions.

As a successfully functioning CAS, a learner can have adaptive capacity. That learner has the ability to respond and find the best alignment with the learning environment. That alignment helps the learner resolve dysfunctional tensions and find coherence. HSD calls this "fitness." The more effectively the student adapts to the world, the more effective he or she is at finding an optimal fitness for each moment.

Other educators have described adaptive capacity in various ways. For example, Michael Fullan lists "capacity-building" as one of four "drivers" that can shift the culture in schools to move toward reform (2016). We agree that this capacity to adapt in response to system change is a critical goal.

> You build adaptive capacity as you use Pattern Logic and Adaptive Action to
> 1) see patterns
> 2) make sense of those patterns
> 3) take action to shift patterns

Over the years, we have learned more about how to set conditions to increase adaptive capacity throughout the system. At this point, we don't have to stop at simply describing the features of adaptive capacity. We also offer an explanation of how the conditions inside the system shape the patterns that create adaptive capacity. We use Pattern Logic and Adaptive Action as a framework for taking steps to increase adaptive capacity of a learning ecology. When Adaptive Action becomes a way of life throughout a system, we say that this system has adaptive capacity.

Adaptive Action and adaptive capacity are at the heart of HSD praxis. They play out in similar ways across a healthy learning ecology. Consider how each of these change agents in the system can engage in praxis, no matter their role:

- ▶ A principal puzzles over ongoing conflicts among teachers on a third-grade team.
- ▶ A counselor puzzles over the lack of response when families are invited to come to school for conferences about their children's progress.
- ▶ A director of food services puzzles over high absenteeism among her staff.
- ▶ A superintendent puzzles over dramatic differences in achievement among middle school campuses, even when the student populations seem similar.

- A student puzzles over the bullying she sees happening on the playground and in the cafeteria.

- A school board puzzles a revision of the school calendar.

Each of these people has a choice. They can continue their current practice and live with the consequences. Or they can use Adaptive Action and Pattern Logic to engage in observation, inquiry, and reflection. They can understand the patterns around them well enough to generate possible options for action and move toward some kind of resolution. Of course, this kind of continual adaptation, learning, and improvement happen best in an organizational culture that supports collaborative inquiry, risk taking, and innovation.

Learning leaders—in both formal and informal relationships—are in a position to encourage collaborative inquiry, risk-taking, creativity, dialogue, and innovation. Classroom teachers, of course, help their students notice patterns in the world around them and patterns in whatever texts they are reading (or composing or viewing or hearing). Instructional coaches stand beside their teacher partners to see, understand, and influence classroom patterns. Administrators—the campus and district lead learners—do the same thing at their scales of influence. Consultants and facilitators also watch for patterns, using strategies and tools to support collaborative inquiry and reflection.

Now how can you use Simple Rules to look back and move forward?

With a group of colleagues or students, talk about the patterns you see in your learning ecology and speculate about what Simple Rules are at work to generate those patterns. Use the forms on the next pages to reflect on your Simple Rules.

Now what will you do to explore your own Simple Rules?

An Invitation to Complex Teaching and Learning

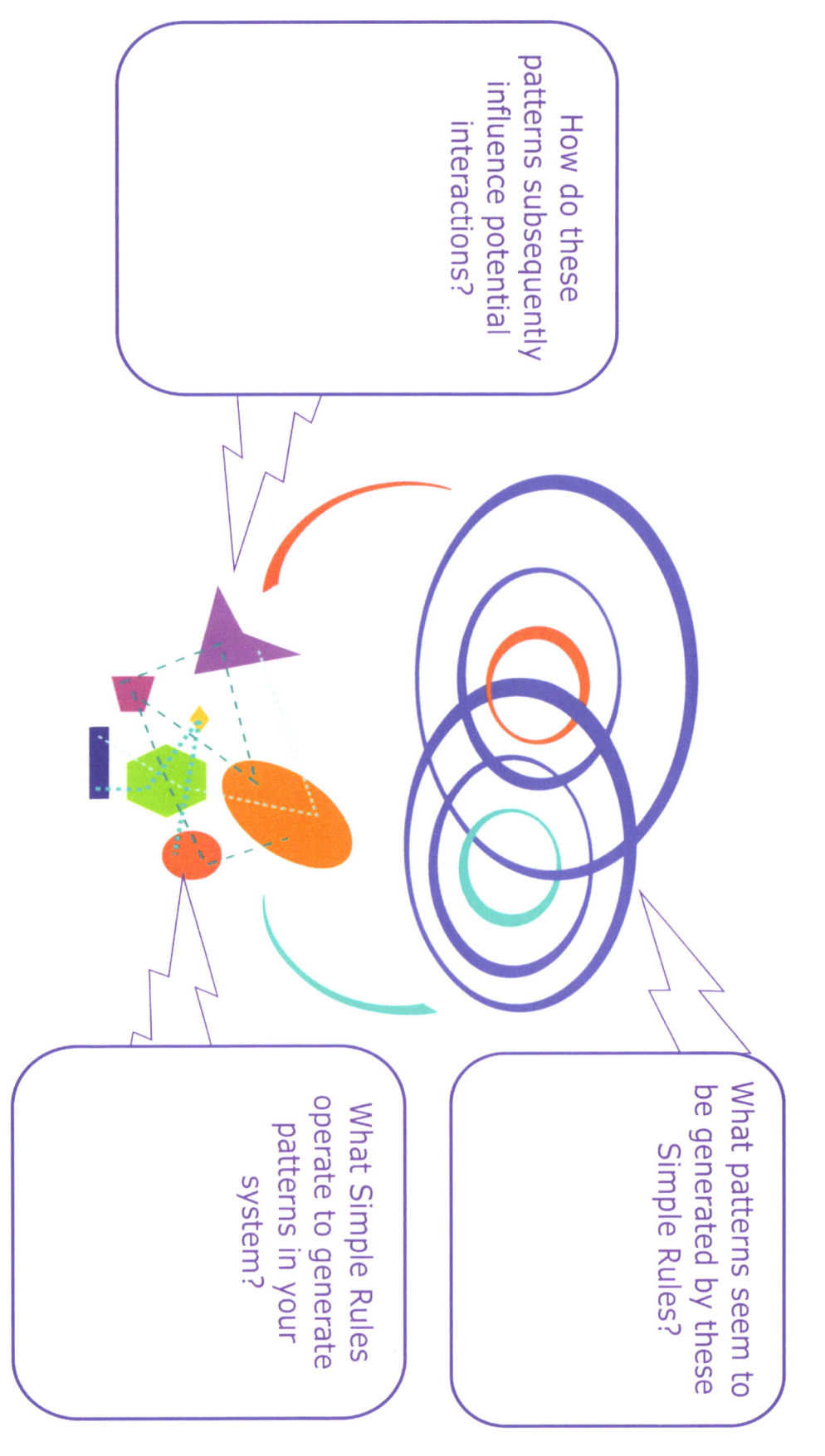

Once you have reflected on your system as it is now, talk about what patterns you would like to see and what Simple Rules might create those patterns.

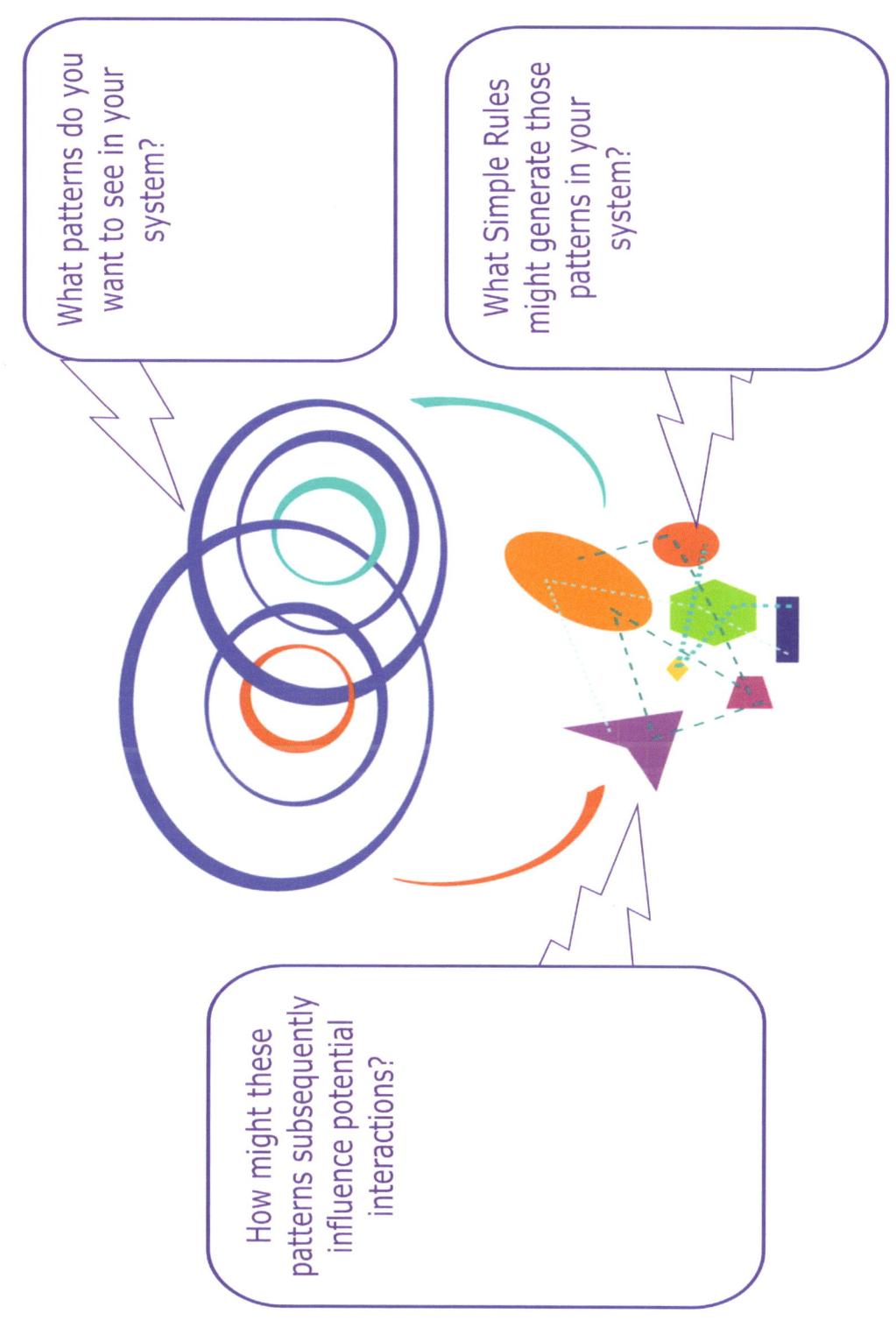

An Invitation to
Complex Teaching and Learning

Finally, consider the HSD Simple Rules and the generative patterns of learning ecologies suggested in this module. How would those Simple Rules and patterns be enacted in your learning ecology? For example, if students followed those Simple Rules, what might be some typical actions?

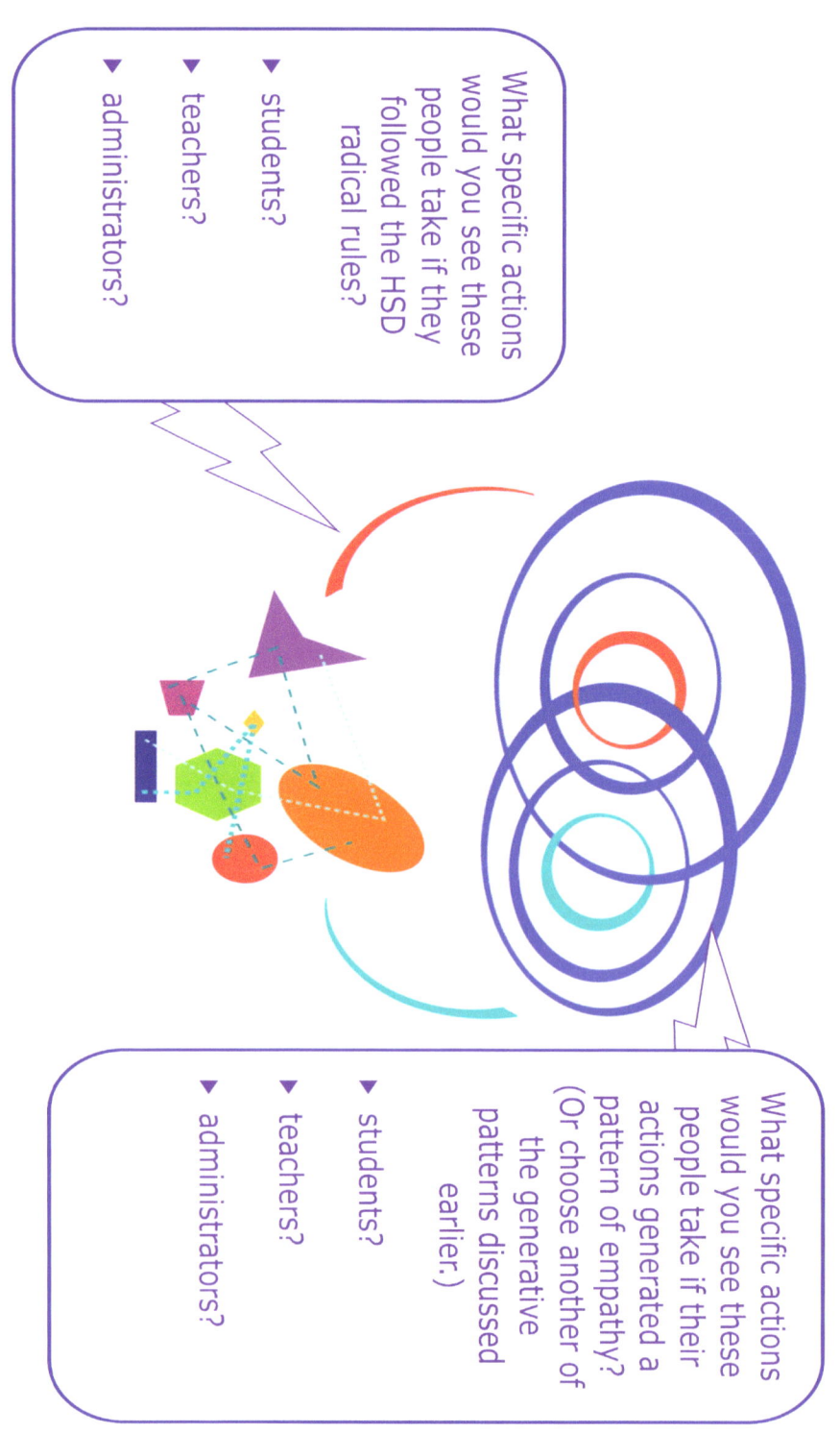

What specific actions would you see these people take if they followed the HSD radical rules?

▼ students?
▼ teachers?
▼ administrators?

What specific actions would you see these people take if their actions generated a pattern of empathy? (Or choose another of the generative patterns discussed earlier.)

▼ students?
▼ teachers?
▼ administrators?

Appendix

References

Books/Journals/Papers

Ballenger, B. (2014). *The curious researcher.* Upper Saddle River, NJ: Pearson.

Carspecken, P. F. (1996). *Critical ethnography in educational research: A theoretical and practical guide.* New York: Routledge.

Cilliers, P. (1998). *Complexity and postmodernism: Understanding complex systems.* London: Routledge.

Clay, M. (1991). *Becoming literate: The construction of inner control.* Portsmouth, NH: Heinemann.

Dooley, K. (1996). A nominal definition of complex adaptive systems. *The Chaos Network, 8*, 1, 2-3.

Dolan P, Leat D, Mazzoli Smith L, Mitra S, Todd L, and Wall K. (2013). *Self-organised learning environments (SOLEs) in an English school: an example of transformative pedagogy.* Online Educational Research Journal. 1-19.

Einstein, A. Quoted in *LIFE Magazine*, 2 May 1955, p. 64, "Death of a Genius"

Elbow, P. and Belanoff, P. (1989). *Sharing and Responding.* New York: Random House.

Eoyang, G. (2012). *Human Systems Dynamics Paradigm Shift (v6)"* Online Resource retrieved 14 May, 2015. (http://www.hsdinstitute.org/resources/hsd-paradigm.html).

Eoyang, G. H. (2002). *Conditions for self-organizing in human systems.* Doctoral dissertation, Union Institute & University, Cincinnati, Ohio, 2002.

Goodman, D. (1999). *The reading detective club: Solving the mysteries of reading/A teacher's guide.* Portsmouth, NH: Heinemann.

Freire, P. (1970, 2000). *Pedagogy of the oppressed.* New York: Bloomsbury Academic, 30th Anniversary edition.

Fullan, M. (2015). *Coherence: The right drivers in action for schools, districts, and systems.* Thousand Oaks, CA: Corwin. Eoyang, G., and Holladay, R. (2013). *Adaptive Action: Leveraging uncertainty in your organization.* Stanford University Press.

Fullan, M. (2011). *Choosing the wrong drivers for whole school reform.* East Melbourne, Victoria: Centre for Strategic Education.

Gell-Mann, M. (1994). *The quark and the jaguar: Adventures in the simple and the complex.* Griffin, IL: St. Martin's.

Holladay, R. and Quade, K. 2008. *Influencing Patterns for Change: A Human Systems Dynamics Primer for Leaders.* Createspace Publishing.

Holladay, R., and Tytel, M. 2011. *Simple Rules: Radical inquiry into self.* Gold Canyon Press. Phoenix, AZ.

Holland, J. (1998). *Emergence: From chaos to order.* Cambridge: Perseus PageBooks.

Kemmis, S. (2010). Research for praxis: Knowing doing. *Pedagogy, culture, & society, 19,* 1, 9-27.

King, Joyce E. "Dysconscious Racism: Ideology, Identity and the Miseducation of Teachers." *The Journal of Negro Education.* Vol. 60, No. 2 (Spring 1991). 133 - 146.

Li, B. L. (2007). Ecological Complexity and Sustainability. http://intersci.ss.uci.edu/wiki/pub/HumanComplexitySeries07Li.pdf

Lave, J. and Wenger, E. (1991). *Situated learning: Legitimate peripheral participation.* New York, NY: Cambridge University Press.

Mayher, J. S. (1990). *Uncommon sense: Theoretical practice in language education.* Portsmouth, NH: Boynton/Cook-Heinemann.

North Star of Texas Writing Project. (2015). *Generative learning patterns.* Unpublished instructional materials.

Ogle, D. (1986). *K-W-L: A teaching model that develops active reading of expository text.* Reading Teacher, 39, 564–570.

Patterson, L., Holladay, R., and Eoyang, G. 2013. *Radical rules for schools: Adaptive action for complex change.* Human Systems Dynamics Institute Press.

Patterson, L., Wickstrom, C., Roberts, J., Araujo, J., and Hoki, C. (2010). Deciding when to step in and when to back off: Culturally mediated Writing Instruction for adolescent English learners. *The Tapestry Journal, 2,* 1, 1-18.

Pearson, P. D. and Gallagher, M. C. (1983). *The instruction of reading comprehension.* Contemporary Educational Psychology, 8, 317–344.

Rothstein, D. (2011). *Make just one change: Teach students to ask their own questions.* Cambridge, MA: Harvard Educational Press.

Smith, F. (1987). *Joining the literacy club: Further essays into education*. Portsmouth, NH: Heinemann.

Stringer, E. (2007). *Action research in education.* Columbus, OH: Pearson Prentice Hall.

Tharp, R.G., and Gallimore, R. (1988). *Rousing minds to life: Teaching, learning, and schooling in social context*. New York, NY: Cambridge University Press.

Vygotsky, L. (1978). *Mind in society: The development of higher psychological processes* (M. Cole, V. John-Steiner, S. Scribner, & E. Souberman, Trans.). Cambridge, MA: Harvard University Press.

Wilhelm, J. (2016). Working toward conscious competence: The power of inquiry for teachers and learners. *Voices from the Middle, 23*, 3, 58-60.

Wink, J. (2010). *Critical pedagogy: Notes from the real world*, 4th Ed. Boston: Pearson.

Websites

Bronke, C. (Retrieved 2016). *http://www.literacyinlearningexchange.org/blog/because-mirrors-have-bias-why-veteran-teacher-works-literacy-coach#comment-1780*

http://www.hsdinstitute.org/
The official website of the Human Systems Dynamics Institute offers a brief overview of the history of HSD, lists of archived resources and training opportunities, a calendar of events, and a list of Associates who are trained HSD Professionals

https://www.facebook.com/pages/North-Star-of-Texas-a-National-Writing-Project-Site/122628771136292
This website is the page where you can find out more about the Writing Project.

Obama, B. (Retrieved 2015). http://www.ed.gov/stem

www.ingramcontent.com/pod-product-compliance
Lightning Source LLC
Chambersburg PA
CBHW041535220426
43663CB00002B/42